# Dancing...
## for a living-two

by
**Don Mirault**

*Updated and Revised*

*Where The Jobs Are*

*What They Pay*

*What Choreographers Want*

*What To Ask*

**Rafter Publishing**
Toluca Lake, California

# Dancing...
## for a living-two

by
**Don Mirault**

Copyright © 1998 by Don Mirault
Printed in the United States of America

Library of Congress Catalog No. 98-091692
ISBN 0-9637864-6-6

***Rafter Publishing***
*11333 Moorpark Street*
*Suite 141*
*Toluca Lake, California 91602*

# Acknowledgments

Thanks to my family – Sheri and puppy Shaq. A special thanks to a terrific editor, Keith Sellon-Wright. Without Keith the book would be unreadable – and we wouldn't have "exotic locales." I would like to thank Junie Osaki for her expertise and negotiations. Most of all, I want to say thank you to the agents, choreographers and entertainment directors that want every dancer to fulfill their dream and know the pure joy of dancing for a living.

Cover Design & Layout by Junie Osaki
Cover Art by Rowen Barnes Murphy

# Table of Contents

# Chapter Three (cont'd)

# Chapter Four –

## Las Vegas .............................................. 51

# Chapter Five –

## Cruise Ships .......................................... 75

# Chapter Six –

## Branson, Missouri .................................. 89

# Introduction

# Time Flies

Imitating life, the world of dance flies by and constantly changes along the way. It's been three years since "Dancing... For A Living" was published, and in that time the dance community has made many significant advancements. The Screen Actors Guild has established new benefits and minimums for dancers with the help of dance agents and The Choreographers Resource Center. More dance magazines have hit the newsstands keeping dancers and teachers informed. A dance network has made its debut on cable and believe it or not, we are represented on the Internet.

I know this may not be the golden era of dance, with hundreds of dancers working in the Ziegfield Follies. I'm also aware that Hollywood isn't putting out a new musical every week. But dance is alive and kicking.

Broadway is breaking box office records and remaking some of the smash hits of the recent past. "Showboat", "Grease", and "How To Succeed In Business Without Really Trying" have all done well and have put many dancers to work.

Foreign dance productions are still going strong, but not in the countries you may think. I will update the information I gave you in "Dancing... For A Living" and talk about work in Japan and, surprisingly, Guam.

Disney has been extremely busy with many tours of "Beauty and the Beast", "Pocahontas", and "Hercules". I've updated the information about Universal Studios, and expanded the theme park workplace to cover Opryland Productions.

Las Vegas will always be Las Vegas, and the major resorts just keep on being built. As long as that keeps happening, the resorts will always need entertainment and that will mean more work for dancers. In this edition we will talk about working at the MGM Grand Hotel.

A landmark in dance and a dream for many young ladies has been the Rockettes. In this book we'll find out just what it takes to make that dream happen.

At the time my first book was printed, finding a dancer represented by an agent was a long shot. Today dance agents are firmly implanted and here to stay. Because they are a major part of the dance landscape, I've dedicated a whole chapter to dance agents and how the dancer who is interested in a dance career can get a hold of one.

In an interview with Zach Reed, President of the Society of Stage Directors and Choreographers, we will focus on what they have accomplished. We will also discuss how they have helped give the dance agent leverage by having the choreographers represented. Also, everyone has heard the expression, "information is power". Well, not only is this true on Wall Street, it's true for the artist. We're going to take a look at the amount of information available to the dancer and let you know how to get it and how to use it. The information provided in this book is to help you get work as a dancer by knowing a little bit about the job and about the choreographer you're auditioning for. The fewer mistakes you make, the better your chances are to make a career of dance. Although this information will help, nothing will take the place of talent, training, preparation and persistence. When you hear entertainment directors, talent supervisors, and choreographers repeat the words, training, personality, appearance, over and over again – take this information to heart, because it's exactly what they need to see from the dancer they're going to hire.

# Chapter One

# A Learning Experience

Every dancer dreams of working with a certain choreographer and I was no exception. I had been a professional dancer for just over a year and I was performing in my second Las Vegas dance review. This was 1980, and the hottest choreographer in the West was a man named Ron Lewis.

Ron Lewis had a style of dance to die for. It was a combination of street and technical dance that is not only rare but exhilarating to perform. He had funky, rhythmic moves that no one else was doing at the time and his creative ideas and use of props were phenomenal. He was well known in Las Vegas for shows like "Casino De Paris", "Viva Les Girls", and "Bare Touch of Vegas", but it was his choreography in Liza Minelli's nightclub act that brought him to national prominence. I didn't care about all that, I just wanted to work for him in the worst way and do that funky jazz style.

I got my chance one day when I read that Ron was going to choreograph a brand new show in Lake Tahoe. The show was called "Hotter and Hotter" and they were looking for male lead dancers, female lead dancers and chorus dancers. The producer was Frederick Apcar, a well-known European man that had produced many shows and was still in charge of the Dunes Hotel and the "Casino De Paris".

I went to the audition.  Ronny's style fit me like a glove and halfway through the call he asked me to leave the stage and go sign a contract with Mr. Apcar.  I almost ran to the Producer's office I was so excited.  When I got there, Mr. Apcar was just getting off the phone and asked me to sit down.  He spoke in a very thick French accent with a low growling voice.  It was not a comfortable situation at all.  Frederick Apcar said, "Ron likes you very much, you're tall, blonde and a very good dancer.  Go to Tahoe, learn his style and I bring you back here to be lead dancer in Casino De Paris.  The show pays $800.00 a week and you will be in rehearsal for eight weeks.  The rehearsal pay is $100.00 a week, you pay for your trip up there and you pay for your housing."

Wow!  $800.00 dollars a week!  But I had just bought a house in Vegas and the thought of trying to pay my bills for two months on $100.00 a week in rehearsal pay was making me very nervous.  I gathered all my nerve and said, "Mr. Apcar, I just bought a house here.  I can't pay for the house plus an apartment in Tahoe on $100.00 dollars a week for eight weeks."

I expected him to say, "Well, maybe we can help with housing", or "Maybe we can get you $200.00 a week rehearsal pay".

You know what he said?  "Thank you."  That's it!  He dismissed me right out of the office.  So much for being tall, blonde, a good dancer, and able to do Ronny's style.  I went home in complete shock.  I consoled myself somewhat with the fact that I'd had a good audition and that I was still a working dancer.

At the show that night one of the other dancers told me who had ended up taking "my" job.  It was a dancer I was familiar with and although he was very good, he was known around town for having quite a temper.  I put the whole experience behind me and didn't think about it again... until I heard that while rehearsing a hat and cane number, this dancer got angry, snapped his cane over his knee and threw Ron Lewis off the stage. I wondered if I would get a phone call. Sure enough, the phone rang. The only thing Mr. Apcar said to me was, "Don, it's only six weeks rehearsal now." That was it. No more money, no housing, not even a "how are you?". I turned him down once again and I never had another chance to work with Ron Lewis.

So what's my point? I want this book to have an impact on you. If you are reading it, you must be interested in having a dance career or guiding someone interested in a career. It's good to keep in mind that very often the people you will be dealing with are shrewd business people whose focus is on making money. In their eyes your talent is simply a vehicle for them to reach their goal. You need to know that your talent and your versatility are your leverage in this "show business" bargain.

You've probably studied dance technique for countless hours. That's great. That work is, of course, essential. It is my hope that this book will add another dimension to your dance education, focusing on the subjects of finding work, getting work, keeping your job and becoming a valuable asset to any show. You need to know what questions to ask and have the nerve to ask them. You can really benefit from knowing what's going on on the other side of your audition.

Let me show you what I mean. The first person I want you to get to know is one of the most dedicated teacher/choreographers of our time. She has inspired many dancers to greatness and she has so much to say to the teacher and dancer of today.

## What It Takes – An Interview With Patsy Swayze

Patsy Swayze is a no-nonsense master teacher, choreographer and director. You may or may not want to hear what Patsy thinks it takes to make it in the dance world, but you have to respect the opinion of a person who has been at the top of dance for well over 40 years.

Patsy has owned and operated dance studios in Houston and Los Angeles. She has choreographed hundreds of musicals and operas, is a tireless speaker at conventions educating both teachers and dancers, and choreographs for film and television.

Here is a little bit of what Patsy has to say:

DM: *Patsy, why is it more difficult to make it as a dancer today than when you started?*

PS:  Well, when I was dancing they were doing lots of musicals. In fact, if you were well trained, in good shape, and decent looking you would work – no doubt. Today, they're not doing many musicals, and there are a lot more dancers competing for far fewer jobs.

DM: *So what would you tell the dancer beginning a dance career?*

PS:  I would tell young dancers what I've always tried to stress in my school. I've always geared my school toward the performing arts, not just dance. A dancer must know dance, voice, drama, how to use their lighting, performance skills, and much more. In Houston I had a semi-professional performing company. Some performances were paid and others weren't, but dancers gained much needed performance experience. All of my dancers performed in operas, high school and college theatre, and professional local theatre. There are many dance schools around the country that feel the way I do. But then again, a lot of schools teach dance and that's it.

DM: *So what do you say to dancer who is currently in a school that only stresses dance?*

PS: Get out! I'm not saying leave the school, unless there's another one near by that stresses performing arts. I'm saying if there isn't, then the dancer must take the initiative to find someone that will help them learn voice, drama, acrobatics, stunt-fighting, whatever. You see, if you stay in a school that just teaches dance, and there are very good schools that have this philosophy for teaching, chances are you will probably be more of a chorus dancer than a principal. I try to teach and create complete performers. Dancers that know how to work, to create characters, sing, sell, and of course, put music in motion, which I call "dancing". I have over three hundred dancers still performing today, most of who are in principal positions in shows such as "Cats", "Les Mis", or they did "A Chorus Line" for the run. They're in Vegas or France, everywhere.

DM: *Name a few dancers we might know.*

PS: Well, of course, my two sons, Patrick and Don, and Patrick's wife Liza. They've just performed on the Music Awards. My daughter, Bambi, performed last year on The Academy Awards. Tommy Tune, Lisa Hartman, Jacqueline Smith have all studied with me and have done well. When you work at becoming a complete performer, your career can go anywhere and people know you're capable of doing whatever is asked of you.

DM: *How does a dancer know when it's time to go to New York or Los Angeles to pursue a career?*

PS: I won't advise a dancer to pursue a career in New York or Los Angeles until they've done everything they possibly can in their local area. You must perform every type of job locally and hope to gain enough experience and maturity to be able to handle the ups and downs of New York or Los Angeles. In New York, you're going to have to compete against a hundred dancers who have been around the block a few times. If you can't handle that, you're just wasting your time.

DM: *You do a lot of choreography. What do you see lacking in today's dancer?*

PS: Discipline, focus and versatility are definitely lacking. I am so tired of dancers telling me at an audition, "I forgot my tap shoes." How do you do that! This is your business. Versatility we've talked about a little bit. Many dancers only do one thing. I don't care if you're a hip-hop dancer and we're doing a hip-hop show. I want an all-around trained dancer. Focus is another thing lacking today. I don't think dancers realize the kind of focus and discipline it takes to make it today. I had a young dancer come up to me and say that she was going to take six months off from dance so she could be a cheerleader. I told her she should just take the rest of her career off because she would never make it. I was a cheerleader in high school, but I never stopped dancing. If you take time off from dance, your career goes backwards because your competition gets better, and you don't.

DM: *Okay, Patsy. Let's say you're at an audition, you've made your first cut and now you're looking at your first group of five dancers. What do you like to see?*

PS: Enthusiasm, energy, attentiveness, and I love to see people walk into a room, well groomed. I don't care what today's styles are. If I'm auditioning for a ballet dancer and you're wearing a thong leotard or baggy pants or jeans and sneakers, I won't even look at you. I try to be very fair with all dancers. I don't care if you're not the best looking dancer in the room, or you're a little too tall or a little too short, I try to give everyone the same shot. My teacher, Marsala Donovan-Perry used to tell me, "This is your business! You wouldn't go on an interview in your sweat pants, then why would you go to an audition dressed down." I look for someone who's on time, who's prepared, who's got the picture and resumé. The first impression you make means a lot. I see dancers that do their combination, go to the side and drink and talk. They don't stay attentive to corrections I make with other dancers that they could apply to themselves. I also look for the reaction and reception I get when I make a comment or correction. If I get a bad attitude to a correction, that immediately tells me not to waste my time with this dancer.

DM: *What else do you look for?*

PS:  Well, dance for me is visual music, so I look for a dancer with a gleam in their eye, who's dancing for the sheer joy of dance. A dancer that has a great sense of musicality – you couldn't throw them off the beat if you wanted to. These things I look for. I know dancers get nervous, but you must channel your nerves into positive energy and make it work for you. Nervousness I can work with, fear I can't. If dancers would stop thinking about trying to get the job and just dance for the sheer joy of dancing, they would get more work and be far less nervous.

DM: *What do you tell your dancers about getting work?*

PS:  I tell my dancers if you have talent and you're persistent and consistent, if you're well educated and well trained, you may lose a few, but you're going to work. I have never known a dancer to follow these guidelines and not work.

*DM: I'm very happy about the fact that teachers and owners of studios have been buying "Dancing... For A Living". What would you tell teachers who want to take their studios to the next level.*

PS:   Today, the competition is so rough. The teacher must continue to educate themselves on the current job market and the needs of choreographers and directors in order to better educate the kids. If they don't, they're gonna see a lot of broken hearts, a lot of frustration and their work go down the drain. It's the same today for the teacher as it is for the dancer. You must continue to study new and different techniques. Up until just a few years ago, I would go to New York every summer to study. I took at ABT with a lot of the great older teachers where I could get that Old World style. I studied with Bob Fosse when he was alive and got a lot of the Jack Cole style. I studied tap with Paul Draper, who is still considered a concert master when it comes to making tap sounds and choreographing to classical music. Don't ever become self-satisfied. Teachers must also be able to advise students when it's time for them to go to New York or Los Angeles. Not just from a job standpoint, but is this dancer a party-kid or a mature person. They need to tell their dancers to take their vitamins, to eat right, to go to auditions every day, to never be satisfied with where they are and constantly push to new levels. A teacher must also know when to say to a student, "you're not ready to go to New York, but if you want to dedicate yourself and do this, this and this, one day you will be ready."

*DM: Is there anything better than having a student call and tell you they've just landed a Broadway show?*

PS:   Nothing!

## Choreographers Resource Center

Zach Reed is the President of the Choreographers Resource Center, an affiliate of the Society of Stage Directors and Choreographers. Zach has been a pioneer in the dance industry. He has helped to make the entertainment industry more aware of the importance of the contribution made by choreographers and dancers.

DM: *How tough was the battle to start this in motion. Did choreographers fight you or did they all sign up.*

ZR: We don't have every choreographer with us, but we have the large majority of choreographers, especially the ones that are really busy in the film and television markets. And no, it wasn't that tough of a fight at all. The community of choreographers are all creators by nature, so it was very easy for them to see the benefit of what we're all trying to accomplish. The time was long overdue for this, especially since choreographers have been making such enormous contributions to the film and television industry for years. They've seen the benefits the SSDC has had and they want to be respected by the industry for the work they do.

DM: *Has it been difficult to gain that respect from the TV and film industry?*

ZR: Yes and no. The independent film producers have been good but sometimes the studios have been difficult in the sense that they'll tell us, "We don't want to deal with the Union, you're not a big enough power." But we get contracts signed and we try to move on.

DM: *What is your main objective and where are you hoping to go?*

ZR: Well, our main goals are to create more work opportunities, elevate community awareness to what we do, and educate the industry and the public. We want them to know the contribution we make to film.

DM: *I can imagine that the agents will be right in there with you?*

ZR: Yes, the agents have had the foresight all along to see that this is going to benefit everyone involved. It will benefit their choreographers and even their dancers down the line.

DM: *Very important, especially to me, is how this affects the dancer.*

ZR: Well, the film and television industry somehow doesn't have respect for "bodies that don't speak". With the unionizing of choreographers and with education about the contribution that dance and choreography makes to the overall quality of a picture, it helps to legitimize the dancer also. They can see the training and abilities that dancers bring to the film.

DM: *It's true –because dancers are "bodies that don't speak" they are considered the same as extras. The truth is that dancers bring many more hours of training and talent to a film.*

ZR: Absolutely. And that is just a part of the education process, of making the industry fully comprehend the value our art form has to the industry.

DM: *Thank you Zach.*

I wanted to introduce you to Zach not only for the wealth of information he has to offer, but to get you to realize that many people are at work on your behalf. They have been diligently working to educate the industry on the hours of training dancers go through to be proficient in their field. They are literally out there gaining respect for you. They are fighting for benefits, minimums and hopefully one day soon, an Academy Award category for the contribution dance makes in film. You will reap the benefits from the work that Zach Reed, Grover Dale and countless others have done. It was not long ago when dancers didn't have minimums. They were paid slightly more than an extra. They didn't get residuals and it was difficult to qualify for benefits. But it's even more than that, it's respect. Not to take anything away from extras, because they work very hard and long hours, but they don't have to train to be an extra. The truth is my Grandmother could be an extra tomorrow if the scene called for an eighty year old woman to knit a sweater on the front porch. The industry needs to be aware of the hours that dancers put into their craft.

A while back, I was dancing on "Murder She Wrote" with about ten other dancers. We had a real nice number with Donald O'Connor, Connie Stevens, Ann Francis and some other stars. At one point the assistant director called for "background" (meaning dancers). "Background" is a term they often use for extras. The dancers, being professional, started to move to the stage. I stopped everyone and told them not to go. Once again, the AD shouted, "background to the stage please". And once again nobody moved. This happened one more time with some anger in the voice. Finally I went out and said, "We're dancers, not background. We've worked very hard to be dancers and as soon as you ask for dancers to the stage, we will be there." He said we were absolutely right and apologized. It was a small step but something that needed to be addressed. Fortunately, we have people like Zach Reed out there addressing these issues.

Okay let's talk about work. Where are the jobs and how do you get them?

# Chapter Two

# Dance Agents

I don't think anything has changed as rapidly in the dance world over the last few years as the acceptance and validity of the dance agent. They have become as important to the dancer as the choreographer used to be not so long ago. A dancer today without representation will find it very difficult to have a satisfying dance career in the LA/NY markets. For this reason, I'm going to talk to a couple of dance agents about what they do and more importantly, about how you can get representation. Since Julie McDonald was first in "Dancing... For A Living", I'm going to start with Theresa Taylor-Campbell of the Bobby Ball Agency. These interviews will not only give you insight into what an agent does and what they look for in a dancer, but you will see a little bit of their personality. This is very important when it comes to agents and choreographers because this is the beginning of a business relationship. A relationship where both people should feel comfortable and confident about the other. The agent must know about you, your strengths and abilities and you must be comfortable enough to tell them.

## Bobby Ball Agency
### Theresa Taylor-Campbell

I wish all dancers could have the presence and impact on stage that Theresa has when you first meet her. You can immediately tell that she's smart, knows her clients, and knows her business. The first question I asked was if I could sit in on an audition. She was kind enough to say "yes", so the next few pages are partly interview and partly observations of this audition.

DM: *In my first book I interviewed Julie McDonald, one of the other major dance agents in town. She said at the time that dance was going through a tough transition period. How is dance doing today?*

TTC: Dance is good! I represent around 300 people. Now before you say "Wow, that's a lot" you have to remember these people are all ages, and specialize in different categories like MTV or commercials or theatrical. I would have to estimate that 100 dancers are booked out at any one time. So from that alone you can see that dance is good. There are a couple reasons for it. The international market is very big right now; it offers dancers a lot of opportunity for work. Cruise ships are doing well and doing a lot of entertainment. Television shows like Drew Carey are doing complete dance numbers weekly and they're using dancers that are more mature. This was unheard of a few years ago. Shorter dancers are working again, and ethnic is still hot. So I have to say dance is good.

DM: *It's so important for dancers to have agents today. I want them to know how they can get represented. How often do you audition for new clients?*

TTC: We hold auditions four times a year, but there are many ways to get our attention. First, send us a picture and resumé. Send us a flyer or postcard about a show you're involved in and if time permits we would love to come. We try to see shows and showcases that dancers are performing in. My staff and I will also watch class periodically to find new talent. We want to find the best talent out there, so if you're well trained and talented you will get seen.

DM: *The audition is so important, let's talk about that. How do you run your audition?*

TTC: I run the audition just like a class. I hire or ask a teacher/choreographer to come in, put the audition together and teach a combination. This particular audition will be run by Janet Roston. Janet teaches class all over town, including the dance department for Beverly Hills High School. She's a terrific choreographer of plays, music videos, and teaching videos. Janet has the patience and personality to make dancers feel comfortable and really show their best.

At the audition, Theresa and Janet started with the young dancers first. The age group was from 7 to 12. Approximately forty dancers in this age group showed up to dance. There were a variety of levels from the very new dancer to some seasoned professionals.

As an observer, I found that the nervousness of the dancers was very obvious; but the little ones hung in there and learned the combination.

DM: *Theresa, what is the most important thing you look for with this young age group?*

TTC: At this age, of course, we like to see some training and discipline, but far and away the most important thing is personality. I have to see the dancer get past their nervousness and show me how much personality and charisma they have. When you think about the types of work they will be up for – and that's our main concern – they have to be able to handle the nerves and strut their stuff.

DM: *Since they are so young, what can you tell the moms to do to help them out?*

TTC:Moms are pretty instinctual.  They usually dress them cute, tell them to smile, and encourage them, which is good.  They should have a picture with them.  It doesn't have to be an 8x10; a snapshot of some kind is good.  Try to get the best quality you can, meaning clarity and good expression.  If the dancer has some type of resumé, that's also helpful but again at this age we don't expect them to have too much.

DM: *Now, I know you have to be very selective and the competition is tough, but out of this particular group of forty young ones how many will you represent?*

TTC:We may only take one or two.

DM: *Wow! That's rough!*

TTC:Well, that's what the average comes down to.  We may take three but at the next audition we might not take any new clients.  Remember, I have many types of dancers already represented and I have an obligation to them.

The next group in was the older dancers – the age range was twelve and higher.  I was looking at a group of about sixty dancers.  I have to say, I thought there would be more.  Some of them looked like professionals that had been working in the business for a while and either didn't have an agent or maybe wanted to change agencies.  Other dancers in the group looked like high school students that wanted to test the market while they're in school and maybe consider a dance career in the future.  Some dancers appeared to be in way over their head.  They were so nervous and *didn't have a clue as to what was expected of them.*

I'm not trying to be cruel, here. My point is that when you haven't had a lot of dance training, it's difficult to be confident in a situation like this. On the other hand, when you're in class five or six times a week and you're used to auditioning, then an audition like this is a breeze. I believe that teachers can really help their older students by running mock auditions in the studio from time to time. Have a friend come in and run the "audition" just like it's the real thing. Give a combination, call the dancers out in small groups and give them feedback at the end of the audition to let them know which dancers you would hire and why.

DM: *Theresa I know this age has to be even more competitive and you have to be more demanding and selective so I'm going to let you go at it and tell them everything you want them to know.*

TTC: Thanks. First of all *study.* Study, study, study. I have to have a well trained, versatile dancer that I can send out in a variety of areas.

*Be on time.* If you're not on time for the audition, how can I expect you to show up on time for a call.

*High energy.* Stay up and focused from the moment you walk in until the moment you leave. You are being evaluated the same way you would be on an audition.

*Be polite, be friendly.* These are things you should know and things that will help you get jobs.

DM: *Sorry to interrupt but I have to say I was amazed at the number of dancers that had what I would call very low energy. They would be day dreaming, yawning or just not paying attention.*

TTC: It's true, and I'm sure they are wondering why they can't get an agent. But you know, it's a lot of little things that really play an important part in this business. Okay, where was I?

*Wear something flattering for the audition.* You should wear something that shows off your best attributes. You can show me the other loose fitting, street style of clothing later, but if you wear really loose fitting clothes, I'm going to assume you have a weight problem. Oh, by the way, weight is major! If you're overweight, start working on it now. Weight is without a doubt the number one reason I can't represent an otherwise good dancer. It's not just my opinion, but people won't hire dancers that are overweight.

*Pictures and resumés.* Again I will accept a Polaroid at the audition if it's all you have. But for the older dancers, if you have an 8x10, make sure you have your resumé stapled to the back. Very often the resumés get separated from the pictures and they don't help the dancer auditioning. If you don't have an in-depth resumé because you haven't had a lot of experience, please be sure to list the training you've had. Let me know who you studied with, what scholarships you've had, what high school or college experience you've had. It all helps.

After everyone learns the combination – and we take our time to make sure everyone learns it – we will then put you into smaller groups. Usually six or eight depending on the size of the room and how many dancers need to dance. When we put you into these groups please listen for your name and for your position . Downstage right, upstage left and so on. Once you find your position, stay in it, so we always know where you are. I'm saying this because sometimes pictures don't always look like the dancer and you can get lost at a large call.

*Sell, sell, sell ,sell, sell!* This is a must. The competition in the dance world is very heavy. Dancers are still auditioning in groups of 250. Smiling and selling is so important on an audition and it's very important here. We will tell the dancers to relax, have fun, and show us your personality over and over again at the audition. It's that important.

*DM: Thank you Theresa.*

I have to say I was amazed at the uninformed dancers. I would guess that sixty percent, and maybe more, didn't fully understand what was taking place at this audition and hadn't a clue as to what was expected of them. Theresa informed me that many dancers with representation could use a seminar on how to audition. Many dancers at this audition had low energy, weren't really paying attention and didn't even know how to find upstage left, or downstage left.

The audition process is the most important part of a dancer's professional career. You must know how to conduct yourself professionally and how to stand out in a positive way. There is a terrific book highlighting this and more called "A Dancers Manual" by Bobby Boling, that I would encourage everyone to read. If you don't know how to conduct yourself at an audition, your chances of finding dance representation are drastically reduced. (Information on how to get that book and others appears at the end of this book.)

Once again, I want to thank Theresa. I also want to let you know that just before this book went to press, Theresa left the Bobby Ball Agency to go into producing. Her assistant, Susan Salgado, has taken over the dance department. Now I want to give you another opinion from an equally respected dance agent. Lets hear what Tony Selznick has to say.

## Kazarian Spencer & Associates
### Tony Selznick

Since this chapter on dance agents is towards the beginning of the book I want you to notice a common theme in the backgrounds and the personalities of the people I introduce to you. They all started as dancers but the important part is they never stopped learning. You will see throughout this book dancers that have continued to grow. Dancers that took the art form seriously, did everything they could to help their careers, and when they were through, went into other dance related businesses. You will meet dancers that own their own dance magazines, created web sites on the Internet or became dance agents. Tony Selznick is one of those driven dancers. He had a terrific dance and acting career. He owns a Production Company with partner Russell Clark. He runs an international dance competition and if all that isn't enough, he is part of the biggest and most respected dance agency in Los Angeles. Tony Selznick, Julie McDonald and Tim O'Brien represent choreographers and handle dancers for Kazarian Spencer & Associates. Together, this is a powerful group of people representing dance. I spoke with Julie in the first book so for this edition I wanted to get Tony's opinions on dance today.

DM: *Tony, how is dance today?*

TS:  Dance is very good, and getting better all the time. Although cruise lines and Las Vegas are doing well, I'm talking primarily about Film and Television. This is my focus and because of films like "Shall We Dance," "The Full Monty" and "Austin Powers," dance is really very good. In Television, "Drew Carey" has ignited a comeback for dancers on TV. His success has sparked other shows like "Friends," "Third Rock from the Sun" and "Dharma and Greg" to use more and more dancers. Jenna Elfman, the lead actress in "Dharma and Greg" is a former dancer and talks about her ballet classes all the time. So, dance in Film and Television is good. I know for your book, you discuss all types of dance work but for me Film, Television and Broadway are tops, and Film and Television is where the residuals are.

DM: *Now, you handle mostly choreographers, right?*

TS: Yes, Tim is head of the dance department and Julie and I handle choreographers. There is a big push now to take choreographers to the next level. Many choreographers are writing and directing film and episodic Television. This is great and it's where we want to go. As choreographers get their projects underway their creativity and their value in the industry gets recognized. This, in the long run, is beneficial for everyone, especially the dancer. With choreographers writing projects, you know there will be dance in there somewhere.

DM: *What do dancers need to do to help prepare themselves for this trend?*

TS: One thing they need to do immediately is to study acting. You know the old cliché that dancers can't act. Well unfortunately it has come true on more than one occasion. When they started casting "Fame LA" they auditioned the dancers first and then the actors. This is very rare in Hollywood. They were hoping to find dancers that can act and solve a multitude of problems. The dancers were terrible. It isn't just that they were bad at acting but you could tell right away at the audition that they didn't have a clue about the process of acting. They just didn't study.

DM: *There are a lot of people trying to get the word out that dancers need to sing, dance, act, roller-skate, do gymnastics, anything and everything possible to make it in this business.*

TS: Exactly. Today's working dancer is versatile. If you're versatile, you don't know where dance will take you. I'm an example. I never thought I would be a dance agent. You know, it isn't over yet. I'm learning so much about the business as an agent that it's helping me to produce my own projects, which is my next step. I'll give you an example of how valuable your training is as a performer. We were recently in Japan with our dance competition and we were giving dancers a combination dance/acting class to build self-esteem, promote creativity and to express ideas. One of the Japanese businessmen said this type of class is given to heads of companies to get them to be creative and express ideas. Our training as performers works well in a lot of areas, if you always continue to learn.

DM: *What should a dancer know about the agent that represents them?*

TS: Trust them! You have to have teamwork and a trust relationship with your agent. We are working for you all the time whether you are busy at the moment or not. Dancers and choreographers to an extent, think that if it's slow and they're not working, that their agent isn't working for them. This is not true and this type of mentality doesn't do any good for anyone. Dancers must work for themselves always. If it is a slow time for you, you should be doing a staged reading, or a showcase, or taking class with as many different choreographers as you can. Get yourself out there where things can happen.

DM: *I know this may not be your area but how hard is it to get represented by Kazarian Spencer and how often do you audition?*

TS: Right, Tim and his assistant, Sohl, really handle that, but it is very difficult to get representation. Another dance agent just left to go into producing and a lot of her dancers scrambled to come over to us, so we are loaded right now. But I have to say that any well trained, persistent dancer can make it happen. Tim auditions about once a month and they watch classes and showcases looking for talented dancers. You can be seen if you train and get yourself out there.

DM: *Tony, I host a competition called "Rainbow Connection". I talk to hundreds of young dancers that love dance and compete almost every weekend. What do you tell your young dancers at "Winners" (a dance competition) about the business and about winning and losing?*

TS: Winning and losing is very healthy if you give it the right amount of importance. Dance is so valuable to young kids. It gives them self-esteem and it lets them know the joy of performing but I see dancers that are angry if they don't always get the high score. This can be very dangerous when you become a professional because, as you know, in this business you are going to lose more than you win. You have to think in terms of becoming better. If your self-esteem is tied to winning every time out, you're going to be very disappointed no matter how good you are. Learn everything you can about dance, acting, and singing. It will all pay off at some point in your career.

DM: *Thank you, Tony.*

If you are considering a career in dance today, you must have an agent. I've given you two valuable opinions from respected dance agents. It is now up to you to find a way to get noticed. Submit your pictures and resumés, go to one of their open calls or invite them to a showcase. You have to take your own career in hand and make it happen. Kazarian Spencer auditions once a month and

Bobby Ball auditions four times a year.  Both agencies told me if you hear about the audition and show up uninvited, you will be seen.  So get prepared, show some initiative and go get a dance agent.  Here are a few agents to submit to in New York and Los Angeles.

**Kazarian Spencer & Assoc.**
11365 Ventura Blvd.
Suite 100
Studio City, CA  91604
(818) 769-9111

**Bobby Ball Agency**
4343 Lankershim Blvd.
Universal City, CA  91602
(818) 506-8188

**Dorothy Day Otis Agency**
499 N.  Canon Dr.
Suite 313-314
Beverly Hills, CA  90210
(310) 887-7028

**Duva-Flack & Assoc.**
200 W.  57th St.  Suite 1008
NYC, NY  10019
(212) 957-9600

# Chapter Three

# Guam and Japan

That's right, Guam!  Surprisingly, there are excellent opportunities for the dancer in Guam.  Working outside of the United States can be sort of an intimidating idea.  However, since Guam is an English-speaking U.S. Territory that uses the U.S. dollar as its currency, there is not as much to be concerned about as you might think.  Japan, on the other hand, used to provide a lot of opportunities, but changes in their economy have reduced the number of imported jobs available for dancers.  In this chapter, I'll point out the things you want to be aware of when considering work in either of these exotic locales.

## GUAM

Dancers are having the time of their life working in "Fantastique", being performed at the SandCastle Entertainment Center in Guam.  Many people in the dance world aren't even aware that Guam is using the talents of American dancers and that they have been for quite some time.  To give you insight into this terrific dance job, I want to tell you about a very special choreographer, Jerry Jackson.  It's very important to know as much as you can about the choreographer, agent or entertainment director that you are auditioning for. It always gives you an advantage to know what their background is, what style they have, and what they expect from the performers they hire. I know this information is difficult to obtain, and that is why I make it a priority to get it to you.

I remember the words of Michael Peters, a choreographer I admired very much, who said, "Don't limit yourself. A versatile dancer is a hot commodity." Well, it makes perfect sense that Jerry Jackson has been a hot commodity for forty years. He is often called the "Renaissance Man" because he has the ability to produce, write, direct, choreograph, design costumes and compose music. How's that for versatility?! Jerry choreographed "Seven Brides for Seven Brothers" on Broadway at the Alvin Theatre. He choreographed the 100th Anniversary of the Folies Bergere, in Paris, France. He has created, directed and choreographed the Folies Bergere in Las Vegas, from 1975 to the present day. This is a successful run no other choreographer can match. He has written, directed and choreographed many revues in Las Vegas, The Bahamas, Australia, Paris, Acapulco, Puerto Rico, Guam, Lebanon, and London. But I don't want to just talk about credits, because I could go on forever.

I want to talk a little bit about background and style. After acquiring a Masters Degree in Art at UCLA, Jerry worked as a regular dancer on the Danny Kaye Show where he met and later assisted Hermes Pan. He later became an assistant choreographer to a dancer many of us have heard of, Mr. Fred Astaire. This is important information. You can imagine that someone with these credentials would be very high on training, discipline and style. I had the pleasure of working for Jerry Jackson at the Folies Bergere in Las Vegas. Now, as dancers, we all learn a little something from every dance opportunity.

Let me tell you how Jerry helped me to become a better dancer.

First, if you don't want to dance with all the energy and enthusiasm you could possibly bring to the stage, don't dance for Jerry. His numbers are fast-paced and high energy but it's more than that. His costume changes, music changes, and set changes are so fast, you're working just as hard backstage as you are onstage. I believe this is one of the reasons for his successful long running shows. The audience is stunned at the amount of visual entertainment being thrown at them in such a short time. Another benefit of fast changes and staging is Jerry can make 30 dancers look like a cast of 100. This is an ability many dance teachers should try to emulate in competitions and recitals.

Second, is the uniqueness of Jerry's style. Like all dancers and choreographers, our style comes from our teachers, choreographers and people we admire. So when you combine that with your own personal touch, you develop your style. As I told you earlier, the influence of Hermes Pan, Fred Astaire, Jack Cole and Jerry's own ability, have created his style. Style is everything. I would wager that I can watch a show in any country in the world and in three counts of eight tell you if Jerry Jackson choreographed this show. It has nothing to do with steps and everything to do with style. About the style, deep plié. Did I say deep plié? No, I meant d e e p   p l i é. A good choreographer will tell you what they are looking for at the beginning of an audition. High energy and deep plié are always the first two things you'll hear when auditioning for a Jackson Production. Make sure you warm up because you can bet you will see some extension work. Jerry is famous for the kick layout, and you can expect to see lots of battements in your routines. What's even more amazing is at sixty-two, he will have better extension and release than you will. So don't even try to beat him, we tried that already. I would also like to recommend that you work on isolations. Jerry is very big on isolation work, and like Mr. Cole will be very creative in using it throughout the show. Arm movements, ribcage isolations and shoulder isolations will also be prevalent in your dance numbers.

One other thing you'll find in every Jerry Jackson Production is acting. To me, this is his best attribute. His dance numbers always tell a story and he demands the dancers be the biggest part of that story. His dances always have a beginning, middle and an end just like a good script. And as a dancer you will always be told where you are in history, what you should be feeling, and what emotion should be coming across to your audience. This was thrilling for me. I was a dancer that didn't just want to smile and sell and I was interested in acting from the start of my career. I feel any dancer doing a Jerry Jackson show will be a more complete artist at the end of the run.

Now, back to Guam. The following is my interview with Jerry Jackson on auditioning for and working in "Fantastique" in Guam. Following the interview I'll tell you a little bit about living and dancing in Guam.

DM: *Jerry, tell me a little about Guam and the SandCastle Theatre.*

JJ:   I did a show there in 1991, it was a Vegas revue type show called "Glitz". Isn't that a terrible name for a show? I thought so, but that's what they wanted to call it and fortunately it was successful. The good part was it was the SandCastle's inaugural show and it ran from 91-95. SandCastle is a fifty million-dollar theatre. This is not a hotel or a casino or anything like that. Dancers should know they'll be performing in a state-of-the-art theatre. Then the producers from Guam asked me if I would do a new show. Choreographers always fight for time and money and this was no exception but we put together our current show, which is called, "Fantastique". Although fantastique is a French word, the show is very much a Las Vegas type revue. They really like the American dancer in Guam and I think that's part of the reason for the success.

DM: *What type of audience comes to see this show? Do the locals come or is it mostly tourists?*

JJ:  I'd have to say both. The locals do come to see the show, remember there are a lot of Americans stationed over there in the armed forces. But I would have to say there are quite a few tourists, mainly from China, Korea, and Japan.

DM: *Tell me about the work schedule and the show.*

JJ:  It's two shows a night, six nights a week and the show runs about an hour and twenty minutes long. There is always one act in the show and it's always a visual act. Right now, we have an illusionist in the show. Everyone seems to be into magic these days. The show is very fast paced. The first twenty minutes just flies by with solid dance, costume and set changes. The start of the show is basically "Old Paris" and "New Paris" and there's a Can Can number. There is a Latin section, with the tango and samba and also a Rio and salsa type dance. I've also incorporated a Broadway number and the dancers will perform a fun fifties number around a 1957 Chevy. But there's a lot more. The dancers will get to perform a variety of styles and dances.

DM: *How large is the cast?*

JJ:  Thirty dancers. Which I make look like more, but it fits the room. The theatre seats 500, and resembles a Vegas showroom. They also have a dinner show and a cocktail show like many of the shows in Las Vegas.

DM: *It's all covered dancing right?    There aren't any topless dancers like Las Vegas.*

JJ:    Right, all covered dancing.

DM: *I want to ask you two questions.  In Japan, they have a problem with age.   They don't want the more mature dancer.   Is that the case with Guam?  And two, in Las Vegas some of the shows want the very tall dancer.  Does Guam have a height minimum?*

JJ:    First, no, there is no problem with age.  No one has ever mentioned any type of age maximum as long as the dancer looks good and takes care of themself. But I have to say that height is starting to become an issue.  I don't know why but lately they seem to be wanting dancers that are a little taller.  In the show now, I know I have female dancers that are 5'3" but they are wanting females to be about 5'6".  For the men it's 5'10".

DM: *What else do you need from a dancer wanting to work Guam?*

JJ:    I need energy and stamina.  Good positive energy. You know, the type of dancer that's fun in rehearsals and fun to be around.  But they also need stamina because this is a fast show and it's twelve shows a week.  I also like new dancers, dancers right out of school that may not have a lot of credits but have a lot of enthusiasm.  I enjoy channeling that energy and helping to develop a terrific performer, so make sure you mention that new dancers are welcome at my auditions.

DM: *Speaking of auditions.  What can we expect?*

JJ:    I'm sure I'm not alone when I say please don't wear anything too baggy.  I need to see your line.  I need to see body placement and I can't see that if you're wearing the current baggy style of clothes.  Ladies, just wear a nice leotard and bring both rubbered heels and jazz shoes. I very seldom need you to bring tap shoes, just jazz shoes and heels. Your makeup should be pretty. What you would wear out on a date, but not too freaky. I can't use you if it's too freaky.

The dance will be a strong jazz combination, ballet and some street. I never do the preparation, pirouette thing that many people do. I don't know what that really tells you about a dancer. I learn more from a strong jazz combination. Of course, I'm looking for technique. There will be turns, extensions; and isolations are very important. I like people that pick up the combinations very quickly. We don't have a lot of time for rehearsals and there are quite a few numbers to learn. I'm always looking for good positive energy.

I watch dancers all the time, so once you walk in the studio, know that you're auditioning. I'll give you an example of what I don't want. When I choreograph I'm always prepared. I have all my choreography ready, but sometimes when you see the routine up and running you have to make changes. When I make changes and I see a dancer rolling their eyes – that's the kind of negative attitude I can't tolerate. I need everyone to be working together for the good of the show.

I remember working with Fred Astaire and Fred was working out a step in the mirror. Out of the corner of his eye he saw one of the chorus ladies frowning and making faces, like Fred couldn't do this simple step. Of course, he could do the step, he was working on something else to go with it. He called me over and said, "You see the girl in the red leotard over there against the wall. Tell her goodbye."

DM: *Where do you audition?*

JJ:    We hold auditions in Las Vegas and Los Angeles. I will also take submissions. You can send a picture and resumé and a video tape. Videos are very helpful and we've hired from them in the past.

No one knows more about creativity and art than Jerry Jackson, but I also wanted you to know what day-to-day life is like when you're a dancer in Guam. Jerry suggested I speak with the entertainment director at the SandCastle Entertainment Center. So I thanked Jerry for his help and followed up on his suggestion.

I contacted Scott Rogers at the SandCastle. Scott is the Entertainment Director in Guam and dancers will work directly with him. He has quite a background in the arts and ran the La Mirada Theater here in California. I asked Scott a few important questions about contracts, pay, and quality of life in Guam.

## Contracts

Yes, all dancers will receive a contract and the initial term is for nine months. It is a standard contract with a few clauses we've talked about before. One, you will have to maintain the same appearance as when you were hired. You cannot change your hairstyle drastically without permission and gaining or losing a large amount of weight isn't acceptable either. All dancers will receive a round trip airline ticket, but if you violate your contract and head home early, you will have to pay your own fare back to the states. After the initial contract, you have the option of re-signing for a period of six months, nine months or even up to a year. Many dancers have enjoyed their time in Guam and decided on the year extension. Of course, final approval will be up to management. I asked about disciplinary action – if dancers were terminated and sent home, or fined or suspended. Scott said, "We've had very little trouble with dancers in Guam. But I have found from the past that a one or two day suspension works the best. I don't fine dancers and then have them work because that's like working for free. But I have suspended dancers for the day, without pay, and let them go back to their apartment and think about it."

## Arriving In Guam

Once you've been hired and you've traveled across the Pacific Ocean. You will be met at the airport and taken to a hotel, where you will stay for one week at no cost to you. The SandCastle will put you up for one week and rent you a car for two weeks, absolutely free. I think that's a nice gesture. You can get your bearings and see a little of the island on your time off. After the one-week period they will assist you in finding an apartment. Of course, with dancers coming and going you could replace a dancer that is headed back to the states. But the choice is yours. You will receive $600 per month for housing. If you decide to get a real nice apartment by yourself and spend the whole $600, you can do that. Or if you'd like to share an apartment and put some of that housing stipend away in savings, you can do that, too. Remember, this is $600 per month above your regular salary. Now to rehearsals.

## Rehearsal and Show Pay

Rehearsals will start right away and you will be paid $50 per day flat rate. Regular show salary is in the $500 dollar a week range but there is a lot of room for advancement. You can understudy the Principal dancers and receive extra money. If you do a cartwheel on stage you can get extra acro-pay. There are dance captains and swing dancers, so the possibility of making extra money is up to you. Again the reward goes to the versatile dancer.

## Lifestyle

I was happy to discover that Guam is not as remote as you might think.  The cost of living is comparable to Hawaii.  A little more expensive than what we might be used to, but not as shocking as Japan.  The area around the theater is a well-known resort area and is filled with tourists.  Like all tourist resorts, it's more expensive. Away from the hotels you can eat and live much more cheaply.  Scott lives almost 45 minutes away from the theater and he tells me prices are reasonable there.

The sound of the word Guam sounds like you're headed back in time to a remote jungle.  Although it is a dense tropical island and has the humidity to go with it, you are not going to miss any of the luxuries of the good old USA.  First run movies are playing at the cinema – the same movies that are currently playing in Los Angeles. They have a Planet Hollywood and Hard Rock Café.  The nightlife is terrific with many modern discotheques including "Onyx" which is right in the SandCastle (dancers from the show get free admission).

As you can imagine the beaches are beautiful and there's a lot to do out on the ocean.  Scott and many other dancers have gotten their diving certification and enjoy scuba diving as often as they can.

## On Class

Scott told me there are a couple of good dance studios.  A few dancers from the show will teach class but guest teachers will also come in from the states and teach. One dancer in the show found an exceptional vocal coach and signed on for another contract mainly because she was improving so much vocally with this particular teacher.

There are a few last things I want to mention about Guam.  Although this is considered a foreign country, it is much easier to work in Guam than it is in Mexico or

Japan.  First, the usual language barrier isn't a problem. The national language is English and Chamorro, with both being taught in the Guam school system.  The dollar is the national currency, so there's no problem with an exchange rate and you can even dial the United States, just by dialing a 1-area code and number.  Just like any other long distance state to state call.

Scott Rogers and SandCastle Entertainment will receive video submissions from dancers and will either hire you if there's an opening, or notify you of the next audition.  You can send a picture, resumé and your dance video to:

**SandCastle Entertainment Complex**
1199 Pale San Vitores Rd.
Tuman, Guam  96911
E-mail:  entmgr@baldyga.com

## JAPAN

I devoted an entire chapter to Japan in "Dancing... for A Living", but as I mentioned at the beginning of this chapter, things have changed there quite a bit.  So I felt it necessary to update the information.  I spoke with Minnie Madden who has produced and choreographed over twenty-one different shows in Japan over the last ten years.  She told me that the situation for American dance shows has never been worse.  Japan is having a very difficult economic time right now and the entertainment industry is having the same downturn as Japan's Nikkei Market.  The Nikkei Market is the equivalent to our Dow Jones.  Their stock market is down and their currency is at an all time low when compared to the American dollar. An American dance show costing one million U.S. dollars just three years ago would cost a million and a half today. That would be for the exact same show and the only difference is the change in the exchange rate between the dollar and the yen. It's a good time for Americans to travel to Japan, but not a good time for Japan to be importing American dance shows. The change in the exchange rate is why I always tell dancers to get their pay in U.S. dollars. It doesn't matter what country you're working in or how stable you think that country is, if you are taking a job in a foreign country make sure your contract says, U.S. dollars or the equivalent of U.S. dollars.

Minnie has informed me that many of the agencies that book American shows have had to branch out into other businesses because of the cost to import. They are now in real estate and travel industries. But don't worry, these exchange rates are cyclical and it will probably change in the near future. Besides, there are many other countries still using American dancers. Countries like Australia, France and U.S. territories like Guam. If you happen to be lucky enough to be offered a show traveling to Japan, consider the information I'm about to cover before you sign your contract. The current exchange rate will help your cost of living a little bit but Japan and especially Tokyo is one of the most expensive places on earth. I will also include some information on the country, and on which personal items you should bring.

## Work

Going to Japan? Take your stamina with you, because if you've accepted a job in Japan be prepared to work. Most shows are seven days a week. You will usually perform three shows a day and you might be able to get one day off a month. Frightening, isn't it? The shows run an hour to an hour and fifteen minutes with two or three acts, but they are fast paced, hard dancing shows. Your rehearsal period will be in two stages. First, a two to three week session in the states where the show will be choreographed and staged. Then, you will travel to Japan and have two or three days on stage to acclimate to lights and sound.

Let me summarize by giving two examples of six-month contracts in Japan. Outside Tokyo the same show will run two to six months, and although you're dancing three shows a day, your rehearsal schedule will be minimal because you're performing the same show. You can expect some brush up or clean up rehearsals. Again, if the attendance is down sometime during the run you may get a day off.

In Tokyo, a show will run for thirty days and will be replaced by a new show *every thirty days*. Now, you have a six month contract, performing three shows a day, seven days a week for thirty days. If that's not hard enough, you will also be rehearsing next month's show sometime during the day. I can hear you moaning! I'm sure you're dying to find out about the money (next section). I'm not kidding when I say Japan is a work-oriented country.

On the bright side, I've talked with many dancers who have worked in Japan and were glad they went. Minnie Madden estimated that out of a hundred people hired for Japan, ninety to ninety-five percent have enjoyed it and would go again.

## Work Visas

You'll of course need a passport for Japan. You will need to relinquish it temporarily to the Japanese Embassy to stamp it and validate your work visa. Like the U.S., the laws on work visas change constantly and keeping up is difficult, but as of this writing the agent in Japan is responsible for your work visa. The visa is valid for six months and no longer. With this particular work visa you are allowed to moonlight in the dance or modeling field, although I can't imagine where you'd find the time or energy.

## Question Your Producer

Remember, your producer in the States is your lifeline of information. *Ask all the questions you can.* Where are you performing? What part of the country? Where are you living? Have they seen it? How many shows a day? How many different shows in the run? How much *money in U.S. dollars?* Minnie Madden has agreed that most producers will tell the truth, good or bad. A producer doesn't want an irritable unhappy dancer in a foreign country. It just means more work for them. You see, if a producer lies to a dancer about the job, it makes it more difficult to find quality dancers to do their next show. It's good business for a producer to tell the truth and it's good business for you to ask all the questions you possibly can before accepting a job in Japan.

## Hostessing

Hostessing has always had a shady, uneasy connotation to it. I think it's because the definition is so vague. It can mean anything from seating people in a restaurant, to social dancing, to prostitution, which leads to white slavery! Oh my God! The young girl went to Japan, they stole her passport, she can't get away and they've forced her into a life of sexual slavery. I think they made a TV Movie of the Week out of that story. I'm sure it did happen somewhere, sometime, but not to dancers performing lounge shows in Japan.

Hostessing may be part of your work commitment. ASK! Find out what is expected of you before and after the show. Japan places a high priority on being polite, courteous and social. Men, women and entire families will want to talk with you, learn things about America and tell you about themselves. It's very important in their culture to be extremely social and hospitable hosts while you're in their country. It's also very prestigious to be seen out on the town with Americans, but don't misunderstand, they are sincere. They may buy you a drink, dinner or give a small gift and expect nothing in return but social grace and good company.

Japan is fascinating in that everything has its place. If a Japanese man is interested in a sensual evening, there's a place for that. There are baths and geisha girls everywhere. If he is interested in a pleasant evening of conversation with a foreigner, that too has its special place. I know this is strange to our way of thinking. Here is a true story that might help as an example.

Susan was dancing in a Tokyo production and one night decided to have a drink after the show with a couple of friends of the producer. She talked with one man in particular for about two hours. The next evening they talked again. They laughed about his broken English, the differences in cultures and were becoming friends. Only at the end of this evening the Japanese man gave Susan a very beautiful watch as a gift. Well, immediately all the warning lights went off in Susan's head. She refused the gift, but when the Japanese man kept insisting, she courteously accepted. Susan was feeling very uncomfortable now and was looking for any excuse to escape. The young man must have sensed her anxiety because the next evening, he met with the producer, called Susan in and gave her another gift. This time he brought his wife and entire family with him. The gesture was to sincerely thank her for being his friend and bringing his family was to prove to her that his intentions were honorable.

You may be asked to hostess between shows or after the show. Find out before you accept the job.

## Money

Income does not always mean cold hard cash.  You must look at the benefits offered with the cash in order to complete the picture.  Here's a comparison example.

In Mexico City the average American dancer can eat very well, very cheaply.  Entertainment is also relatively inexpensive, so when a producer in Mexico offers $400 a week and a hotel room, that's not such a bad deal.  In Tokyo, one of the most expensive cities in the world, that won't cut it.  The Japanese producers adapt this way.  Most jobs going to Japan will pay $350 – $450 U.S. dollars a week, but they will enhance your income by paying for your room and board.  Board will include two meals a day.  Everyone I talked with felt there was always good food available and plenty of it.  In any other country, you might say, "So what!  I'll pay for my own food and eat what I like."  In any other country you might be right, but Japan is home to the $7 cup of coffee, $15 beer and $13 ham sandwich.  Board can be the most important benefit negotiated in your contact.  In fact, if board is not offered as part of your compensation for working in Japan, I would strongly suggest not taking the job.  Without board, you will spend almost your total salary just to eat.  In Japan, a quarter–pounder with cheese at McDonald's is just over $10.

Another incredible benefit while working Japan is medical coverage.  Hotels and nightclubs are bonded medically for all employees, *this includes you*.  I know of dancers who have injured themselves on the job.  They were immediately taken to the hospital, treated and escorted home.  All costs, medications, and transportation expenses for follow up care were covered.  There was even compensation while injured or ill.  When you consider how few non–union dance jobs have any type of medical coverage, this is quite a plus.  I want to make you aware of how invaluable some benefits can be.

## Lifestyle

To enjoy Japan it might help if you know a little history and even a little geography. Relax, I'll keep it short. Japan is a lovely land with magnificent mountain ranges principally due to its volcanic origin. Japan is densely populated with over 120 million people, 12 million living in Tokyo alone. There are four major islands, Honshu, Kyushu, Hokkaido and Shikoku. Three quarters of the entire population live on the main island of Honshu. The major cities on this island are Tokyo, Yokohama, Kyoto, Kobe, Osaka and Nagoya. These cities are modern, sophisticated and crowded. Japan's population is sixth in the world. That's 120 million people in an area about the size of Montana.

Even though Japan cannot feed itself fully, it has the distinction of producing more food per acre than any other country. Japan boasts the world's largest fishing fleet, nearly one–half million boats. Understandably, fish replaces meat in most dishes. Meat prices are staggering!

## Currency

The unit of currency in Japan is the Yen, (¥). Bills are 500, 1000, 5000 and 10,000 Yen. Coins are 1, 5, 10, 50, 100 and 500 Yen. Since 1971, by agreement with the United States and Japan the Yen has been allowed to float. The exchange rate from dollars to Yen changes constantly.

## Subways

Tokyo, Osaka and Nagoya all have safe and clean subway systems. This is a highly developed public transport system that is convenient and inexpensive. The subway station entrances are usually marked in Japanese and English. On the first floor you will find ticket offices, fare maps, fare machines and the ticket barrier leading downstairs to the second floor and subway platform. You may be nervous and confused at first, but once you get used to using the subway system, it really is the best way to get around.

## Mail

You can find English speaking personnel at the customs office and at most International Post Offices. They are open from 8 AM to 8 PM. Stamps may be bought at hotels, post offices and at any small shop that displays a red and white double capped T. Red postboxes are for ordinary mail, blue ones for 'express' mail or special delivery. In Tokyo if there are two slots on the red box, the right-hand one is for Tokyo, left for everywhere else. Air mail to the USA or Europe will take six to nine days.

## Credit Cards, Traveler's Checks

All major credit cards and traveler's checks are accepted in the larger establishments. American Express, for example, is accepted in over 3,200 establishments. Most of the western style hotels and shops will exchange traveler's checks, U.S. dollars and pounds sterling. The use of personal checks or cashier checks is not advised as it is time consuming (clearance can take up to three weeks) and involves much red tape.

## Tipping

A charming courtesy in Japan is that you never slip money to anyone without first wrapping it in something, a paper napkin, a bit of paper, an envelope. This includes tips to waitresses, doormen or bellhops. Never try to tip someone who has given you directions or done a kindness, they would feel insulted. Just thank them warmly. Sidewalk shoeshine boys build in their own tips by charging foreigners more than they do Japanese. Don't give them more than they ask.

## Packing List

Minnie Madden has prepared a packing list that is given to every cast member prior to leaving for Japan. Look over the list. Some things to think about. Fishnets and nylons for tall women are difficult if not impossible to find in Japan. Bring extra! A towel in Japan is a little larger than our washcloth. You might need four towels to dry off. Bring your own!

### Suggested Packing List

| | |
|---|---|
| Dance Shoes | Rehearsal Wear |
| Character (1) | Personal G–string(s) |
| (plus backup if available) | Stage Makeup (lashes) |
| Jazz Shoes | Hair equipment (pins, spray, |
| Fishnets (suntan 2 pair) | rubber bands, etc.) |

### Toiletries

| | |
|---|---|
| Towel/Washcloth | Sweater(s) |
| Laundry Soap | Jacket |
| Iron (1 per group) | 1–2 Evening Wear (dress) |
| Alarm Clock | Warm comfortable clothes |
| Tapes/Recorder | Camera/Battery/Film |
| Books/Magazines/Stationery | Optional |
| Pajamas/Slipper/Robe | Scissors, tape |
| Comfortable shoes | Aspirin/Midol |
| (easy to take off and put on) | Sewing Kit |
| Umbrella | Dramamine/Gum (for plane) |
| Hat/Gloves/Scarf | |

## Class

Like everything else, class in Japan is intense! It's very competitive, not only for the dancer, but between schools.

There are four major dance schools in Tokyo:

**Broadway Dance Center**
**Ichi Bunga**
**Professional Dance Center**
**IBC**

These studios are always competing to be the best school with the best teachers, facilities and stereo equipment. One of the reasons the schools are so competitive is because they sell memberships to their dancers. It's the same way we might join a health club or a country club.

Dancers are loyal to one studio, paying a membership fee for a year. Membership fees are expensive, but don't worry, a visiting dancer is able to pay for one class at a time. The individual class fee is usually around $20. This is a little higher than what we're used to paying, but many schools give discounts to American dancers working in their country.

Let me tell you one reason that classes in Japan are so expensive. The competition between major schools is so great, they'll pay well-known American teacher/choreographers top dollar to teach at their school.

Jaymi Marshall, an excellent choreographer and a good friend is paid $1700 a week to teach one or two classes a day. This is far more than he could make in the states. Jaymi told me the major schools have at least one well known American teacher working for them at any given time. Some American teacher/choreographers go to Japan once or twice a year for 4 to 6 weeks at a time. Now, don't get me wrong. Unlike Mexico, the Japanese teachers are qualified, up to date and able to teach you new styles and steps. The Japanese dancers are also capable of performing on the same level as American dancers. Japanese studios are complete, offering jazz, ballet, tap, hip hop, traditional Japanese dances, everything. You can consider taking class in Japan a plus if you're going there to work.

## OTHER FOREIGN COUNTRIES

In this chapter we've discussed issues relating to working in two foreign countries. Many other countries, such as Australia, Mexico, and France, are utilizing the talents of American dancers. Although I won't go into specific details here about the issues that you might face when working in these countries, keep in mind the following things when you're considering work abroad:

Have a valid passport and keep it with you. (You may have to relinquish it briefly to the producer so that he/she can get your work visa. This should only take a day at the most. Demand it back after that. It's your passport!)

Take a major credit card with you. Make sure this credit card isn't max'd to your limit. The reason you're taking this card is not so you can buy more souvenirs – it's just in case the producer closes the show, cancels your return ticket, and keeps your last check. (Don't scoff. It happened to me in Mexico.)

Fire precautions. Whenever traveling to a foreign country, you'll most likely find yourself in a hotel room. Know your fire exits. I've been awakened in the middle of the night by a maid screaming "fire" in a foreign language. It wasn't until I saw the smoke in the room that I realized what was happening. Confusion can be fatal.

When venturing out to see the sights in a foreign city, take another cast member with you. Large cities in foreign countries have the same crime problems we do here, and an American tourist is easy to spot.

# Chapter Four

# Las Vegas

Las Vegas still considers itself to be the entertainment capitol of the world  In the last five years six new mega-resorts have been built, including Monte Carlo Resort, the MGM Grand Hotel, New York, New York, Stratosphere, Luxor, and others.  As of this writing, Bellagio is scheduled to open soon – a huge resort catering to high rollers.  The great news is that these resorts will always need entertainment and that means lots of work for dancers.  In this edition we will talk about working at the largest hotel in the world, the MGM Grand Hotel.

## MGM Grand Hotel

Following is an interview with Chris Coaley, Director of Entertainment at the MGM Grand Hotel and Theme Park.  Chris has been a dancer/choreographer for many years and is an inspiration for dancers that dream of moving up from dancer to line captain, to putting together their own small shows and eventually becoming a terrific choreographer.  This dream is Chris Coaley's resumé.  He came up through the ranks, always interested in bettering himself, and that has brought him to this position today.  I worked with Chris years ago in the "Folies Bergere" and

I'm very happy to see his incredible progress.   Our interview went like this.

DM: *Tell me, how many different types of shows are you in charge of right now that use dancers?*

CC: Well, first off we have the Grandmosphere.  These are a group of dancers that are really street performers who go throughout the theme park doing a variety of shows.  We also have a couple of theaters that I hire dancers for.  One is the Pirate Stunt Show; we hire dancers and, of course, stunt performers.  Another theater has a presentation called "Unbelievable"; we use dancers in that.  And then we do four large specials a year and I'm always looking for dancers and new talent.  Last, but not least, we have what we call the hotel and casino dancers and singers, and they're always doing short presentations and special promotions throughout the hotel and casino.

DM: *I've seen the Grandmosphere performers in the park. They're very good and very busy!   How many different shows do they do?*

CC: They do five different shows.  The original group did eight, so you can imagine all they had to learn.  That was more musical theater oriented; now we've gone to a more contemporary style of show.  You know, the hip-hop style and disco style.

DM: *So it changes all the time?*

CC: Absolutely.  It depends what the public wants.

DM: *Yeah, I think I saw the Christmas show.*

CC: Oh yeah, that was part of our special event and I think we had seven different street shows going on at that time including a 40's show.

DM: *That is a lot of different shows using a lot of dancers.
How often do you audition?*

CC: To tell you the truth, we audition constantly. If
someone calls up and happens to be in town and
wants to audition, we will audition them. But we
have three large scheduled auditions a year. One in
March, one in the middle of summer and then one
around November for the big Christmas holiday.

DM: *What direction is dance taking at the MGM? Do
you see dancers working more and more into the
future?*

CC: The MGM has really decided now to place a new tag
on the hotel. They are calling it "MGM - The City
of Entertainment", and they've spent a half a million
dollars to realize what that city of entertainment is.
So I think we'll constantly be doing different shows.

DM: *Alright, give me a few examples of how hard these
dancers will be working and how many shows a day
in the different productions.*

CC: Well, for example the theater show "Unbelievable"
does three shows a day, the Pirate show does four
shows a day and the "Grandmosphere" does 15
minute shows and they will do up to eleven shows a
day. The dancers in the Hotel/Casino do a 10 to 15
minute show and they're on this MGM cart. It's
this elaborate car with its own lights and sound, and
the dancers will be brought in to the casino, do a 10
minute show to draw attention and then lead right
into a new slot promotion. So we're using
entertainment to bring attention to a new casino
experience. They also do a real fun bell hop show
right there in the lobby of the hotel for guests as
they're checking in.

DM: *Okay, I want dancers to always know what's
expected of them, so lets use the "Grandmosphere" as*

*an example. They will do eleven 15 minute shows a day. How many different shows will they do?*

CC:  Usually four or five. Let me give you their schedule for today. They will do an eleven-thirty Elvis show. It contains all Elvis music and an impersonator in the front, and the dancers will dance behind him. Then they will change, come back and do a twelve o'clock country show, which is a 10 minute show. Change clothes, come back and do a grove flashback show (like a 60's &70's flashback show) at twelve-thirty, which is a thirteen minute show. Then they'll have a good 45 minute break, do another Elvis show, have lunch and so on. The schedule varies slightly from day to day.

DM:  *How long are they in the park? Is it a full eight-hour day?*

CC:  Yes, eight hours, our hours are 9:30 to 5:30.

DM:  *I'm always looking for work where the dancers don't get bored doing the same show and where there is room for advancement. Is this the case at the MGM?*

CC:  Yes, well, dancers always move around in different shows in the park and in the hotel. But I have to tell you, the theater shows are sub-contracted and they're not MGM employees so our dancers can't go in and out of those shows.

DM:  *What about longevity? Can a dancer work for as long as they like or is it a six-month run and you're out?*

CC:  Well Larry Lee at the Tropicana was my boss for a good part of my career and I find myself taking his approach. If you do a good job and you're happy here, then I like keeping you here. But, if you start slipping and letting your performance suffer then we're going to have to talk about it.

*DM: So who checks the shows and the dancers? Do you go out into the park and watch?*

CC: I have supervisors for every show and they let me know about any problems with the show or with the dancers.

*DM: Las Vegas has always been a great place to work for a couple of reasons: longevity and benefits. For the employees of the MGM, how are the benefits?*

CC: The benefits are terrific. Dancers get all the benefits that other MGM employees get... except one.

*DM: Which is?*

CC: "Guarantee of fairness".

*DM: That sounds pretty nasty. A dancer doesn't receive a guarantee of fairness?*

CC: Wait, they get every other benefit such as great 401K benefits, great health benefits, everything the other employees get. The benefits are the best in Las Vegas and maybe the States, but they don't get guarantee of fairness. Because they are contracted performers there is not a guarantee of fairness. Now what that means is this. Lets say this one dancer, we'll call him Barry, has a certain musical theater look. But I'm changing the direction of the shows to a real street, contemporary look. He just doesn't fit where I'm heading so I'm going to have to terminate his contract and he's let go. He can't now go to MGM and say this isn't fair, because it now becomes the direction of the show that's more important than the individual. Now you can see why the other employees, like a maid or a registration clerk have that clause because their job doesn't change but a dancer's does.

*DM: Does a dancer start receiving their health benefits right from day one or is there an evaluation period?*

CC: It's pretty much like any other company. There is a three-month probation period where we evaluate their performance and either decide that they are right for the MGM or that we've made a mistake.

DM: *I always try to let the dancer know what type of dancer is working at a particular job. What type of dancer are you hiring at the MGM?*

CC: Well I've noticed over the last four years that we really have two types of dancers here at the MGM. I'm not going to talk about abilities right now, just type.
We have the new performer, which is really fun to have with us because they have lots of energy. They're really excited about the job, but they're a little raw so you can mold them a little and help them become better. And because they are in the corporate environment they can grow as an employee as well as a dancer. What's also interesting about the young, new performer is they're here for a contract or two and then they're off wanting to try something else. Then you have the very experienced dancer that wants to stay in one place, make a good salary, establish credit, buy a house, you know, have a real life. Right now, I have about half of each type.

DM: *How long is your contract? Six months?*

CC: Yes, six months.

DM: *What about the elements? Like I said, I saw the "Grandmosphere" performers right before Christmas and it was pretty cold, and I know how hot Vegas can get. So how do the dancers handle the elements?*

CC: Well, you know honestly the first thing that sends dancers away is wanting to try something new. The second thing would be the heat and the cold, not so much the cold but the heat. Remember though, that Las Vegas is just beautiful most of the time.

Now, the hotel performers don't have to worry about the temperature – just the theme park performers. They actually love the cold because dance is so physical that it's easy to get out there and jump around where you don't even feel the cold, but the heat is tough.

DM: *So how do you help them handle the heat?*

CC: Well first we try to costume them accordingly where everything is really breathable and not much of it. We usually lighten up on their scheduling, where we'll have two shows with more of a break, rather than four shows right together. So they'll have more time to cool off. They also have what we call cool ties. They're like these little ties that you throw in the freezer and then wrap them around your neck and they stay cool for about four hours.

DM: *So you wear them under your costume?*

CC: You can even where them over the costume and just make it part of the costume. We also make sure there is plenty of water in the dressing area and breaks. And that's it.

DM: *All right, Chris, what about the audition. First of all, do you advertise to announce the audition?*

CC: We used to put big ads in the regular newspaper but we were getting too many levels of people, not as well trained as we'd like. So now it's just word of mouth and ads in the dance magazines or trades like the Dirt Alert. Also remember, we'll audition people just about any time if they're in town.

DM: *One thing I want to let dancers know is what auditions are right for them. So tell me, what is the audition like and what are you really looking for?*

CC: What we try to do is this. Of course it's against the law to say we want this height or look, but we like to let the dancer know what kind of skills we're looking for. Our advertising for "Grandmosphere" might read, 'Male and female singer/dancers, bring instrumental tape or a capella, bring picture and resumé, looking for strong contemporary voice, must hip-hop'. That way if you don't do those things then you should know not to come. Now for the hotel performers, they don't need to hip-hop. So it might say, 'musical theater background, must sing, strong jazz a plus'.

DM: *When they are choosing a song is it different for each job?*

CC: Absolutely, "Grandmosphere" I want to hear something pop, and for the hotel I want to hear something musical theater. We are always very specific and they should pay attention to that.

DM: *What about the look?*

CC: Again they are two different looks. "Grandmosphere" I'm looking for a youthful contemporary look but you know some of our more mature dancers fit very well into that so its not just about a young look but a young enthusiasm and energy. We have had dancers in their late thirties work perfectly out there in the theme park because of their energy and attitude. But I really like to mix it up. I like unique looks. Let me explain. Remember this is a theme park and I'm dealing with a corporate image, so I do need a clean-cut look. That doesn't mean everyone has to look like college preppies. I like different looks, we have a black dancer with blonde hair and some other very wild contemporary looks, but still clean and well put together. The other thing to remember is that we have had many dancers working in the theme park that were spotted by other entertainment people and have gotten other work. One of our singers is now a principal singer in the EFX show and she got that from the theme park.

DM: *That's always good for a dancer to know that they can advance to another show from this show. I know EFX hires a lot of dancers.*

CC: Yes. That happened recently where a very good dancer came to me and said she wasn't handling the environment very well and could she audition for EFX. I said, "of course" and it was easy for her to transfer from one job to another. She still has to go through the audition but it's easier for a dancer that's already an employee.

DM: *Tell me a common mistake that dancers make at auditions, or what I like to call horror stories. You know, stories about when something goes wrong so the rest of us can learn from it.*

CC: The worst horror stories are when people just don't have the particular level of talent that we need. There are dancers that want to be in the business but they haven't realistically evaluated their own ability. That's the hardest part of the job for me. I don't want to crush their dream, but they just don't have the training and ability to be in the business. So you let them go through the process but they aren't going to make it in the business unless they devote a lot more time to study.

DM: *I try to tell dancers that all the time. Be realistic about your own ability. Know your strengths and weaknesses and work on your weaknesses. What else?*

CC: Being unprepared. I would say only twenty-five percent of the dancers that show up to audition are really prepared. Of course, you have to have talent but presentation is the most important thing. Be confident, present yourself well and go wanting the job. I like to see those things. Make sure you're stretched out before we start the audition. Think about your song selection. I see a lot of dancers and singers choose the wrong song. It's out of their range, or they're doing a belt song in their head voice. I've even seen them audition with the words on a piece of paper in their hand. I think that's being unprepared. If you can't learn the words to a song for the audition, how can I trust you to learn eight different shows?

DM: *If I had to pin you down on experience, what would you say is the level of experience you're looking for.*

CC: Well, that's really hard because it of course depends on teachers and natural ability, but I would like everyone to know that if you don't have some sort of solid training behind you, don't even come.

DM: *What about clothes at the audition?*

CC: You see, that's really difficult too, because we had this guy come in and he was a phenomenal dancer but it was hard to get past the fact that the crotch of his pants went down to his knees and there were holes all over. He had a tattered tee shirt on that looked like he wore it for five weeks straight, and a beard that wasn't trimmed or styled or anything, and old, old sneakers. You know, the total grunge look. I asked for double pirouettes and he was doing four every time. He was terrific. His performance side, though, really suffered. He just wasn't a very good performer and I couldn't hire him even though he was a great dancer. I just couldn't get past the look. I think the look might even work in the theme park. But if this is who this person is, can I count on him to take care of himself well enough to work with the public in the theme park? It's something I have to consider.

DM: *What type of combinations will you give at the audition?*

CC: We'll usually do three combinations. Jazz, hip-hop, and sometimes tap is included too.

DM: *I always try to stress the importance of singing to dancers. How important is singing to this job?*

CC: Very important. They must at the very least be able to carry a tune. If they can't carry a tune, I usually can't hire them for this job.

DM: *For the ladies. Heels, no heels, street makeup, stage makeup, what do you like to see?*

CC: I'll tell you, shoes for the ladies have never mattered to me. If they like to wear heels, fine. If they like to wear jazz shoes or even some boots, that's fine, whatever they dance well in. I don't have any desire to see stage makeup at auditions so a nice street makeup is great. Now remember, that's for the kind of work we do here. Other places in Vegas may definitely want you in stage makeup.

DM: *Sure and that's exactly the kind of thing I want dancers to know about different jobs.*

CC: That's great! I can't stress enough that dancers should know what the job is and know who your boss is before you audition. I'm not saying know your boss well, but know what he or she likes in style and taste and you'll be much better off.

I want to thank Chris for his time and expertise. I also want to tell you some things I found out about compensation. Chris did not feel comfortable talking about pay and I respect that, so I talked to a few of the dancers working at the MGM. Everyone I talked to has enjoyed their experience working there, they love the health benefits and they would recommend the job to others. But they did say the heat can be terrible in the summer even with the precautions taken by management. This is something to consider if you have a low tolerance for working in the heat.

Since we've been using "Grandmosphere" dancers as our example, we'll start with them. Depending on the versatility, experience and amount of seniority you have at the theme park, dancers made between $480 and $600 a week. That's pretty average for a theme park and also middle of the road for Las Vegas revues. The initial rehearsal period and ongoing rehearsals are paid on the same hourly wage. When you think about it, if your working in the park and rehearsing a special event show at night, you can make close to a thousand a week. You'll be exhausted but making some money.

If you're interested in the stunt shows, they make between 35 and 50 dollars per show. (That's $140 to $200 dollars a day for people that don't like to do the math.)

The hotel/casino dancers and singers make about the same as "Grandmosphere" but more toward the lower end of the scale and if you're interested in wearing a character suit, like Popeye, the Cowardly lion and others, they make around $360 to $400 dollars a week.

Remember the particulars I always ask you to consider when taking a dance job. Consider the money, health and retirement benefits, and the amount of fun I can have with this job. Can I take class and continue to improve as a performer? Can I advance here at this job and can I get my next job while working. If you consider all these benefits and the lifestyle that Las Vegas has to offer then the MGM might be a terrific dance job for you. Before we leave the Las Vegas chapter I want to show you a brief section of a contract. I'm going to cover the highlights of a typical production contract. Although they do vary slightly, I think this is a good example of the quality and quantity of work expected of a dancer in a production show. Remember this is only an example. The contract we'll be looking into is actually seven pages long.

## 1. DUTIES AND TERM OF EMPLOYMENT

Employee hereby accepts employment with employer under the direction, supervision, and control of Employer and the Employer's Director of Entertainment for the period commencing...

*This section will state the type of dancer position hired for and the length of time that your contract is valid. Most production show contracts are six months but may be up to one year in length. An example in assumption of this section might read; "Employee hereby accepts employment as a Regular Covered Dancer commencing February 1, 1998 and terminating July 31, 1998."*

## 2. PERFORMANCES

Employee shall be required to perform two or three shows nightly, or up to thirteen shows in a six-day week with one day off. Employee is also required to attend up to three hours of "brush–up" rehearsal. Unused brush–up rehearsal hours are accruable over the duration of the show (or contract).

*This really means if you don't rehearse this week, next week the producer could rehearse you six hours without additional pay. Since no one keeps track of these "unused brush–up" rehearsal hours, a producer could conceivably call you in at any time for any number of hours rehearsal.*

## 3. PUBLICITY

Employee shall make themselves available for any and all publicity, and is not entitled to any compensation, fees, royalties, or other remuneration.

*Simply put, you will perform any publicity the employer deems advantageous to the hotel for your regular salary and nothing more.*

### 4. PERFORMANCE STANDARD

Employee will perform their duties in accordance with the highest standards of quality. The Director of Entertainment will continuously monitor the show and have absolute discretion in insuring that such standards of quality are maintained. Failure to maintain such performance standards is a breach of contract and good cause for termination.

*This means the Entertainment Director's opinion is law, as to whether your performance level is equal to that of your fellow dancers. If he or she feels it's not, you could be fired.*

### 5. PERSONAL APPEARANCE

Employee agrees to maintain the same weight and general appearance that existed at the time employee was hired.

*EXAMPLE: If you gain weight you'll be given a weight notice and weighed. You'll then be given a certain amount of time to lose weight or face the possibility of termination. Oh yes, if you're thinking about getting a tattoo on your forehead and putting a ring in your nose after you're hired, THINK AGAIN!*

### 6. REPORTING FOR PERFORMANCES

*There is a half–hour call before most shows. You must sign in at least a half–hour before a* *performance or rehearsal. If you're late you could be assessed a $25 fine. Three late arrivals during the term of this contract may be cause for dismissal.*

## 7. EXCLUSIVITY

Employee hereby agrees that during the term of this Agreement Employee will render Employee's sole and exclusive services in the entertainment business and media, whether on stage or in moving pictures or on radio or television or otherwise, TO EMPLOYER ONLY, and will not render any such services nor appear publicly for any other person, firm or corporation without first obtaining the written consent of the Director of Entertainment.

*The Employers of most production shows are very lenient with this clause. I know of many dancers, including myself who have moonlighted frequently in other types of entertainment (commercials, movies, conventions). This clause is the Employers protection of their show. I have seen Entertainment Directors come down hard on dancers who work another job all day, only to call in sick for the show at night, or their performance at night suffers because of fatigue from working the extra job. This is an example of how a few dancers have spoiled it for many. Although it's very seldom used, remember this clause is in the contract and you could be terminated for performing in another type of work in the entertainment business without written consent.*

## 8. TERMINATION OF AGREEMENT

This Agreement may be terminated by employer AT ANY TIME, WITHOUT CAUSE, upon two weeks prior written notice to employee.

*(Please read section eight in connection with section nine).*

## 9. LIQUIDATED DAMAGES

Employee recognizes and agrees that Employer may incur substantial expenses in employing employee including advertising, auditions, rehearsal pay and fitting and purchase of costumes and accessories, and that the total damages to Employer resulting from a breach or early termination of this Agreement by Employee are difficult to ascertain, and this Employee agrees to pay to Employer the sum of ($1,500) as liquidated damages.

*Simply put, under this six-month agreement, the dancer may be terminated with or without cause. But, if the dancer decides to quit before the contract is completed, he or she may have to pay the employer $1,500 in "liquidating damages."*

*It's kind of like going to the bank and being assessed a penalty for early withdrawal for taking out your money. No kidding, this is very important if you're not sure you can commit to the job for the length of the contract. I've known dancers who could have done Broadway shows or other much higher paying jobs, but were faced with the choice of turning them down or coming up with $1,500 in "damages."*

These are just some of the highlights in one example of a production show contract. I know hundreds of dancers who have enjoyed working production shows for many years. It is not my intention to steer you away from or toward this type of work, but I do want you to know as much as possible about every type of dance job you may become involved in.

## LIFESTYLE

Once again, under the heading of lifestyle there are many advantages and disadvantages to working in Las Vegas. In the hopes of being objective, which is very difficult since I lived there for nine years, let me explain some of the things you will come in contact with and let you ultimately decide if these are positives or negatives.

Vegas is a very exciting 24-hour town, and that does take some getting used to. Restaurants, bars, supermarkets and even some dry cleaners stay open 24 hours. Entertainment is continuous from 1 PM to early into the morning hours. The casinos, of course, never close. I've had my hair cut in a salon at 3 AM, although today, I can't for the life of me remember why. Everything seems to be completely unconcerned with time.

Vegas seems to have the best of both worlds. Travel just outside of town and experience the small town feel of a desert community. Slow pace, quiet stillness, desert wildlife are all available, if that's for you. Lake Mead, about 30 minutes away, is the largest man–made lake in the United States. Swimming, fishing, boating, skiing and wind–surfing are activities for people who live in this supposedly barren wasteland. Mt. Charleston, just 50 minutes northwest has beautiful hiking in the summer and a challenging ski resort in the winter.

In town, big name entertainment is everywhere. Celine Dion, Cher, Diana Ross, and Garth Brooks are just a few of the headliners. Big time concerts, national rodeo finals, ballooning, off road racing, boxing, ballet, and so many more activities I couldn't possibly name them all. Vegas lifestyle has a lot to offer.


## Credit

Establishing credit for a dancer can range anywhere from difficult to impossible. The nature of dancing in the entertainment field is so sporadic and unsure. Look at a typical hard working dance career.

You work a show in Los Angeles for six weeks but it closes because the backers pulled out. You don't work for a week. You pick up two days work on a music video. You don't work for two weeks. You finally land a job that takes you to Japan for two months. Another two weeks unemployed. Get the picture? When you're trying to explain that type of career to a loan officer at a bank, they stare at you as if you were asking them to finance the space shuttle. One of the great benefits to working a Las Vegas production show is longevity. Some of these shows have been running continuously for twenty years, and although they go through various changes or "editions", if you're good you can be assured of working long enough to establish a good credit rating. There is no other place in the States where you'll find more dancers working continuously for five to ten years and buying new cars and nice homes on credit. Some long time Vegas dancers feel they may have compromised some things in their career by working Vegas, but this type of lifestyle has more than made up for it.

## Housing and Cost of Living

Las Vegas is growing rapidly, and construction of apartments and housing is keeping pace with this rapid growth. This boom in construction has helped keep the cost of housing in Vegas relatively low in comparison to NY or LA. Let me give you a very general example of housing costs in the three cities. In LA a one bedroom apartment in a good neighborhood will run about $650 a month, in NYC somewhere around $1,100 and in Vegas with pool, Jacuzzi, and cable TV, $500-$550 a month. Again, this is just an example and you can get great deals everywhere, if you're lucky and diligent. The point is that housing, both renting or buying is far less in Vegas than in the Big Apple or the Big Orange and that is something to think about.

Food is another example. Though I haven't noticed any real differences in the supermarkets, the casinos are always enticing people to gamble by offering some of the best prices on food you will ever see. Complete breakfast buffets for $.49 and it's not surprising to have a huge prime rib dinner for $3.95. Gawd, this sounds like a commercial, but I want you to have as much insight as possible when you're making career decisions.

But this is not a travelogue. The purpose of this book is to inform both sides, good and bad.

If you have a compulsive personality or if moderation is a word that you're not familiar with, Las Vegas can be a disaster area. Gambling is everywhere, twenty-four hours a day, every day of the year. It's exciting, it's fun, and it's glamorized heavily by the corporations who own the casino resorts. I've had friends get into serious financial trouble gambling. They cash their paycheck, and proceed to spend it all that night, gambling. The next morning they need to borrow money for rent, bills or food. Oh sure, some people do win lots of money, but the truth is, they've built a very large city on the losers. For the vacationer who loses some money and returns home this is not a problem. But for the compulsive local who has the ability to gamble everyday of his life, this can be frightening. It can be far worse than a drug problem, because it's legal.

I am very happy to report that since the writing of "Dancing... For A Living", drugs being used backstage have fallen off dramatically. There are many reasons for this. One reason is, there is now mandatory drug testing when you sign your contract. Oh yes. Don't be surprised if it's not the urine test but the more in-depth "hair test". You'll be asked to give a few strands of your hair for testing. Unlike the urine test, which can detect drugs used in the last 24 to 48 hours, the hair test can detect drug use for the last 4 to 6 weeks. Another reason may just be that the trend is down nationwide on certain drugs, so drug use backstage is down as well. One last reason may be that dancers realize drugs don't help their performance and they really hurt their longevity. Whatever the reason, I am pleased to announce that right now the cycle is in a downtrend and hopefully, it will stay there. Alcohol problems are much more prevalent in Las Vegas. You say, how can that be? Well, anytime you're gambling in a casino, you drink free. If you gamble all night, and many people do, you drink free all night. Another difference is, in most towns the bars close at 1 or 2 AM, but in Vegas there is a small tavern on almost every corner and they don't know the meaning of the word "closed."

I mentioned in the beginning of this chapter that I would try to discuss both sides and let you ultimately decide if Vegas is for you. The truth is, if you're a career minded dancer with common sense and some restraint, then Las Vegas is a great place to live and work.

## Class

Another benefit to working in Las Vegas is the abundance of quality instructors in a variety of dance classes. Don't take this for granted. On a cruise ship or in a foreign show it's very difficult to take class, but in Las Vegas you can keep up your technique, learn new styles, and become a better dancer while you're working. The dance class is the lifeline of the dancer, and as discussed earlier, dance class for the professional is invaluable. Every dancer knows how important class is to their dance abilities, but learning the styles of established and up and coming choreographers who teach class is equally as important. A choreographer is holding an audition and he recognizes you from his class. You already have an advantage. He knows you study, that you're hard working and you're capable of performing his style of dance.

## The Billboard

The billboard of a dance studio is the number one place for finding new work. If I'm producing a show the first place I post the audition information is on the billboard of a dance studio. Why? I want dancers who are studying and sharp, and the word of mouth is going to ensure a good turnout. The billboard with audition information reinforces the benefits of working in a job where you can take class. Don't follow me? Look!

Every dancer knows the benefits of dance class:

To keep technique sharp;

To learn new styles of dance from different teachers;

To hear about auditions for dance jobs.

These benefits are important to your career as a dancer. In fact, I want you to think of your ability to take class as a positive or negative when you consider accepting a certain type of dance job. Example: you're working on a cruise ship and although you're having a good time and making decent money, the chances of you taking class are minimal. But let's say the cast is very career minded and one of the more experienced dancers decides to give everyone a good workout. This is great! You'll keep your technique sharp, but because the ship is so isolated from the dance world, it's very difficult to set up your next job while working.

Consider dance class to be another benefit to working in Las Vegas. Vegas has many quality studios with terrific teachers, but the point is you'll be able to audition for other dance jobs while working. Everyone knows it's always easier to get a job when you already have a job. Many dance troupes and Broadway tours come through Las Vegas and you'll be able to audition for these higher paying jobs. Many dancers have landed Broadway shows while working in Las Vegas, myself included.

In summation, I feel class in Las Vegas is clearly a plus. To make studying easier, here is a list of some quality dance studios, complete with addresses and phone numbers.

**Backstage Studios**
1952½ E. Sahara
457–7310

**Henry Le Tang Professional Dance**
953 E Sahara Ave #35B
892-8499

**Dance Fusion**
1775 E Tropicana Ave
795-3332

**Las Vegas Dance Theatre**
3248 Civic Center Drive
649–3932

**Backstage Studios**
3425 S Lamb Blvd.
739-1446

**Fern Adair Conservatory**
3265 E. Patrick
458–7575

**Rainbow School of Dance**
21 N. Mojave Road
384–6268

**Inez Mourning Studio One Dance**
4601 W Sahara Ave #J
364-2077

**Maliza's Studios**
4133 W. Charleston
870–5508

**Robert Allen Studios**
3977 Vegas Valley Dr.1
431-8441

**Academy of Nevada Dance**
4634 S. Maryland Parkway
798–2989

**Helene Gregory Talent Center**
3755 E. Desert Inn Road
451–1666

**UNLV Dept. of Dance**
739–3827

**London Dance Academy**
4000 Boulder Highway
456–5334

**Dance Charisma**
6000 Spring Mountain Rd #2
364-8700

# Chapter Five

# Cruise Ships

The cruise industry is still at it, enjoying record numbers of passengers and adding new ships and destinations continuously. The great news for us is that the passengers will always need entertainment while they're aboard. Since this is a new edition, let's start with a brand new cruise line.

As I'm writing this particular section, dancers are being hired and getting ready to start rehearsal on the premier voyage of The Disney Cruise Lines. That's right, Disney has decided to put a package together where families and friends can enjoy a couple days at DisneyWorld and Epcot Center and then travel a short distance to board a brand new cruise ship and enjoy a four day sail. The cruise will head to the Bahamas, to a private island Disney owns, and then cruise back up the coast of Florida.

I will have to update Disney Cruises in the future because everything was so new. I had many questions that didn't have answers yet. But the one thing I can tell you is that choreographer Ron DeVito and fellow choreographer Rich Bittner are very excited about putting these three different shows together and having a long and successful run on board two brand new ships. The inaugural ship called Disney Magic will be making its first transatlantic voyage from Florence, Italy to Florida in February 98. The second ship, called Disney Wonder, will sail approximately a year later.

I spoke with Rich Bittner, a terrific choreographer and an old friend about this amazing opportunity for him and a cast of entertainers.

DM: *Rich, you've been dancing and choreographing for Disney for quite while. What role are you playing in this particular project?*

RB:  I'll be choreographing, I'll be assisting Ron DeVito, and I'm acting as a Casting Consultant. All those roles.

DM: *So, give me a little feel for the cruise line. Will there be Disney characters all over the place just like Disneyland?*

RB:  Oh yeah. Not only will there be characters in the three major shows, but there'll be a show just for the characters and they'll be all around the ship.

DM: *Take us through the process for the dancer. Where did you audition, and how many dancers did you hire?*

RB:  We have twenty-two entertainers in the cast and we auditioned all over. Of course, we auditioned here in Florida. We went to NYC, LA Chicago, Miami/Ft. Lauderdale, Toronto and London – which really makes this an international cast.

DM: *How was the turnout?*

RB:  Very good. Really good in NY, a little slower in a couple of cities probably due to some advertising problems, but we were very happy with the turnout.

DM: *You advertised in local papers and trade papers?*

RB:   Yes. Especially in NY, it was all over Backstage (a New York trade paper). We also had a great turnout in Ft. Lauderdale.

DM: *Great! It's almost like a local job for them. They don't have to travel like dancers from LA or Toronto.*

RB:   Exactly.

DM: *Tell me what you were looking for and what the most difficult part of casting was.*

RB:   There are twenty-two in the cast. Ten to twelve are dancers and the others are principals. The shows are going to be very fable oriented with dance, song, and a storyline. So the difficult part was that we needed very talented, very versatile dancers because not only did they have to be triple threats (sing, dance and act) but also they had to be the right type for the principal roles. Every dancer will understudy a principal role. So you can see they had to be incredibly gifted.

DM: *What type of combination did you give the dancers at this audition.*

RB:   The audition was held just like any other audition. We gave two musical theater jazz combinations and one that was a little more hip-hop. Then everyone had to sing.

DM: *Everyone?*

RB:   Yes, everyone had to sing and in this particular job, it's not just carry a tune, it's SING. All the shows are live and we need dancers that sing. You need an up-tempo song and a ballad. We like to hear at least sixteen bars of music but we never stopped anyone if they really wanted to perform their whole song.

DM: *What about tap or ballet combinations?*

RB:  No ballet combinations, but we did throw together a
     real quick tap combo if there was time.  If not, I
     would ask the dancers if they tapped and what
     they've done.  From that you can get a feel if they
     tap or not.  Tap is just for one show, there's a sailor
     number and basically it's just for the guys.

DM:  *What is the ratio of male to female dancers?  Are
     there more women that men?*

RB:  No, it's exactly even.

DM:  *One of the reasons I write this type of book is so
     dancers can prepare for a job like this.  Is it your
     feeling that the most frustrating thing was dancers
     coming in unprepared?*

RB:  Yes that's true.  It usually isn't with the dance
     section, most dancers are ready for that, but with
     the singing, which in this case is equally as
     important.  They would only prepare one song or
     they wouldn't know all the words to the song.  In
     the paper the audition is very specific as to what we
     need to hear, so it's good for dancers to know they
     can't get by with less.  Take it as seriously as you
     would the jazz combination.

DM:  *Some choreographers say it isn't important to pick up
     the combination fast, just as long as they get it.  Is
     that the case with you?*

RB:  No, I need to see them get it and get it quickly.
     With Disney productions there is always a shortage
     of time.  A lot to do in a short amount of time.

DM:  *Okay, you've hired the dancers you wanted.  Now,
     I've seen the information packet that employees for
     DisneyWorld get before they start.  Is it the same for
     the cruise line?*

RB:  They get an information packet that is so complete it's unbelievable.  It has times, dates and places – everything right down to haircuts.

DM: *They fly you in from whatever city you auditioned in?*

RB:  Yes, they fly you in, you stay in a private three-floor townhouse.  It's a large privately owned townhouse but you will have to share it with one or two other dancers.

DM: *Where are rehearsals held?*

RB:  All rehearsals are in the Bahamas.  Because this is the first cruise for a brand new ship, we will all fly to Italy and rehearse in the dock while the ship is being finished.  We can rehearse on the stage and we will be able to run through the show as we cross the Atlantic.  When we arrive in Florida everyone will be up and ready to go.

DM: *What else should they know to prepare themselves for a job like this?*

RB:  Let me think.  All dancers need a passport.  I don't think there are any physicals or medical evaluations, but I can check.  They don't have to weigh-in like on some cruise lines but, of course, they will have to watch their weight during the six-month contract.

DM: *A lot of dancers don't understand that you can really put on the pounds while you're out to sea or visiting the islands.*

RB:  Right.  It's just common sense that we want you to stay with the same look and appearance that you were hired with.  In fact, some of the characters are a little bigger than others, so it's fine for certain people.  But you have to remember they are spending thousands of dollars on costumes, so you have to maintain whatever weight you were hired with.

DM: *So, no blue Mohawks once you take the job?*

RB:  No.  Personally, I think its funny, but no.

DM: *Tell me about the showroom.*

RB:  Well, I've only seen the models and diagrams but as always with Disney, it is state-of-the-art.  It'll seat 1,000 people in regular theater seating, as opposed to cocktail seating, and it has no obstructed views.

DM: *That's great.  So many cruise lines have obstructed views in their showrooms because, as you can imagine, they were built cruise ship first, and entertainment second.*

RB:  The stage for me is the best part.  There is nothing like it on cruise ships today.  We're talking full hydraulics for sets and scenery, front and rear projection, forty-foot fly space, great sound system, the works.

DM: *With a room like that you can do almost any type of show.  What's the scale of this show?*

RB:  The level of the shows will be between a theme park show and a Broadway show, leaning a little more towards the Broadway end.  They will be exciting to watch, especially with the room we have and the talent we have.

DM: *All original shows or will you do other book shows?*

RB:  All original, and they'll be fable-esque types of shows with new and old characters.  Now when I say characters, I don't necessarily mean Mickey or Donald Duck, I mean other types of fable characters.

DM: *And these are the characters the dancers will understudy?*

RB:  Yes.  That's why they really need to act, too.  You see, not only do they have to act and look like these new characters but they may have to do a Jasmine or an Ariel also. It's difficult.

DM: *Wow. And these dancers will be doing three different shows during this four-day cruise. One show each night.*

RB: Right. The ship holds three thousand passengers, the theater holds one thousand passengers. So one show will be performed three times each night and the passengers will all see a new show each night.

DM: *So the dancer hired will be doing three performances every night. How long is the show?*

RB: About forty-five minutes. With probably a half-hour to an hour break between shows.

DM: *I know on many ships dancers not only perform at night but also have some type of crew duty during the day. It's usually a ping pong tournament or water volleyball.*

RB: No, not on Disney Cruise Lines. There are no cruise duties.

DM: *That's great. What about their living arrangements?*

RB: Each dancer will have their own room. They won't have to share a room like on other lines.

DM: *Is it a crew cabin or a regular passenger cabin.*

RB: That I don't know, but I do know they have their own cabin, complete with a TV, VCR and I believe a small refrigerator.

DM: *That's pretty nice. I'll make sure dancers ask if it's a passenger cabin and to find out if their room has a porthole. I know it doesn't sound that important, but if you're onboard for a while you'll really come to appreciate that window. I imagine if you're a dancer with Disney, you better like kids. I'm sure you expect a lot of kids on this cruise – especially compared to other cruises that are very much geared to adults.*

RB:     Oh yeah, lots of children. In fact there are decks of the ship geared specifically for children, and I'm talking about one for toddlers and another area for teens and older kids.

DM:     *How about a casino for adults like other cruise lines or adult getaway areas.*

RB:     No casino, but there are adult only restaurants and night clubs, things like that. There really is something for everyone.

DM:     *Okay, getting back to the amount of work for the dancer. This is a four-day cruise but is it continuous?*

RB:     Yes, that's a good point and a lot of dancers don't understand this part. First of all, they will sign a six-month contract. This first group is signing nine-month contracts but that's because of the three-month rehearsal period. Dancers from now on will sign for six months, but the cruise is continuous. On the fourth day you will arrive into Cape Canaveral early in the morning. One group of passengers will disembark and that afternoon a new group will come aboard. You will have this day to do some things on shore in the Cocoa Beach area. You can make your personal phone calls and do your banking, but it's really your only time off.

DM:     *I'm glad you mentioned that. The work schedule isn't that strenuous, but you don't have any complete days off during the six-month contract. Okay, I always ask this, but it is important. Is the dancer working directly for Disney with all the benefits other Disney employees have?*

RB:  Yes, they have a full health plan right from the start. I don't know if they have a 401K or some type of retirement plan, but I'm sure it's in the information packet.  I do know that the benefit package is fantastic.

DM:  *I know this is a touchy subject especially with Disney but can you give me an estimate of what the dancers will make.  That is, allowing for line captains or swing dancers?*

RB:  This could be subject to change but the dancers will make around $700 dollars a week.

DM:  *The principals will make more?*

RB:  Yes.

DM:  *So if after the first contract one of the principals decides not to stay on, another dancer may be able to move up?*

RB:  Yes, of course that's a possibility.  It's just so new right now that I haven't really thought that far ahead.

DM:  *I ask that because I always feel that a job with room for advancement both monetarily and as a performer is a great job.*

RB:  Absolutely.  You know, what's funny is that there's always room for advancement to other careers on the ship.  I've known dancers that love the cruise ship and may not want to entertain any longer and they become cruise directors, trainers or shore excursion directors.

DM:  *That's great.  I never thought of that.  Well, good luck with this terrific project and thanks for your help.*

Rich will be a terrific addition to the Disney Cruise Line and a great choreographer contact for you to make. Now I want to include some information that is pertinent to all cruise lines and exactly what you need to know before leaving the shore.

## Banking

A cruise ship has almost a full service bank on board and you will have your own account. I say almost because I don't think they have everything, especially in the way of investment banking. Your checks can be directly deposited into your account and you can draw on that money anytime. Take full advantage of using your account to save money. It's difficult to find your next dance job from the ship, so the money you save will help a lot when you head back home. Many dancers have saved a lot of money, returned home for a year or two and decided to do another six-month contract.

## Drill Precautions

You may be cruising on a thousand-foot vessel, ten stories high, weighing hundreds of tons, but when you're in a storm in the middle of the ocean, you won't believe how insignificant you feel. Take drill seriously.

At least once per cruise you will practice lifeboat drills. Every passenger and staff member has a seat on a lifeboat. Your lifeboat number and directions to it are on the backside of your cabin door. As a staff member you may have another duty before heading to your lifeboat. It may be assisting passengers with their life jackets. You will be well trained on drill and your duties. Pay attention, it could be very important. Occasionally, the Coast Guard will hold a drill onboard and evaluate the ship.

## Class

Not being able to audition for other jobs while you're working and not being able to take class are negatives of cruising, but you can adjust.

Although you won't be able to study with other choreographers, you can stay in great shape onboard. There is always a core of dedicated dancers who want to excel at their craft. When I worked the ships there was a well-trained dancer, superior to the rest of us, who would give us a good workout and combination two or three times a week. It was great! We would make it more fun by each creating a few counts of eight of the dance combination. I would take the first two counts of eight then the next person would pick it up and add their own two counts of eight. There is also a full warm up, physically and vocally before every performance. Bottom line, if you want to stay in shape, you can do it on the ship, but meeting new choreographers and learning their styles will have to wait till you get home.

## Drugs

For those of you that don't do drugs you can skip this section, but if you do, you better think again before you bring them on the ship. If you are caught with drugs, the least that will happen is you'll be sent home, but there is always the chance you'll have charges brought against you.

Three things to think about:

1. There are crewmembers that are informants.

2. The ship I went on had periodic drug searches where drug-sniffing dogs were brought through the cabins.

3. On the Islands in the Caribbean a few passengers and crew were foolish enough to purchase marijuana. They would get about a block away and

be arrested. It's a big scam on the Islands where
someone sells you pot and his brother the cop
arrests you. The cop scares the hell out of you,
makes you pay a large fine and lets you go. He
gives the pot back to his brother and they do it
again to the next fool!

## Tid-Bits

The Shore Excursion director is in charge of shore
tours in all ports of call. These tours may consist of
horseback riding, boat rides, hiking to a waterfall, or seeing
the pyramids. The passengers will usually pay extra for
shore excursions. Get to know the shore excursion
director! Many times if there is room available you can go
on the tour for free. While I'm on the subject, it's
important to treat not just the cast but fellow crew
members with courtesy and respect. The crew notices
that you are a crewmember with special benefits and
sometimes they resent that. If you're friendly and
appreciative to your fellow crewmembers, you'll find they
can make your life much easier. Once, the cast did a
special show late at night for crewmembers not on duty.
Not only was it well received, but for weeks,
complimentary drinks would come my way or a cook
would place an extra lobster tail on my plate. What goes
around, comes around.

## Stage

Dancers always have to adjust to different stages, but
how often do you work on a moving stage? Forgot about
that, huh? This is something you may never get used to.
Some nights the water is calm and the dancing is easy, but
some nights it's difficult to keep your balance standing
still. Try a pirouette! Leaps and jumps are difficult for
two reasons:

1. When you leap into the air the stage is not in the same place when you land. Sometimes it's closer—sometimes it's farther away.

2. The other problem I had with leaps is the low ceiling. Remember this is a cruise ship first, an entertainment center second. I would jump into the air and hit my hands on the lights. Also, be careful if you're involved in lifts. You may not have this problem on Disney ships but be aware of it on other lines.

## Questions to Ask

Whatever cruise line you're considering, the answers to the following questions are imperative.

Salary
Rehearsal Pay and Per Diem
Work Duty
Living Arrangements
Eating Arrangements

For more information on Disney Cruise Lines call:

407-566-7577

# Chapter Six

# Branson, Missouri

Through the years, dancers have had to travel to New York City or Los Angeles to make a living as a dancer. This is primarily still the case if you want to be a Broadway dancer or perform in film and commercials. There is no middle ground with cities like New York or Los Angeles, people either love them or hate them. Most dancers enjoy going to New York to take class and see a few Broadway shows and most love the energy and excitement of the city, but some dancers are overwhelmed by the size of the city. Dancers can find themselves in culture shock when they discover the number of dancers auditioning for each part. Many only tolerate Los Angeles or New York because the work is there but cannot imagine raising a family in the city.

I've lived in both cities and enjoyed them both for different reasons. New York was very good to me, I worked quite a bit and there is nothing on earth as exciting as working in a Broadway show. The other side is, a car is very expensive to own in the city, so consequently you're always on the street walking to or from the subway. This can wear on you when the weather's bad or when you're in a hurry and all the street people want to talk. I remember when I first arrived in

New York. I was so excited I was about to bust. An old friend of mine who had been living in the city for a while said, "If I don't get out of here this weekend I don't know what I'm going to do". At the time I thought she was being a little dramatic but after about six months, I was starting to feel the same way.

I guess my point is that even though we all love dance, we are all very different people. Fortunately, we're living in a time when we can have our cake and eat it too. Today, there are other options for the dancer that wants to work and still enjoy a more laid back type of lifestyle. Nashville, Orlando, Las Vegas, and many other smaller cities are hiring dancers. These cities now offer the chance at a career with longevity, benefits and what some people would consider a more "normal" life.

There is also a small town in the middle of the Ozark Mountains that is offering another option for hundreds of dancers. That small town is Branson. Branson has grown rapidly over the last six or seven years. This town in Missouri has over forty theaters showcasing talent six nights a week from March to December. In this chapter, I'll give you two examples of shows that are running in Branson, "Country Tonite" and "Legends In Concert". We'll find out just what is going on in the middle of the Ozark Mountains.

## COUNTRY TONITE

As always, I want to give you as much information as I can about the person you will be auditioning for. I was fortunate to get some background on choreographer John Burdette and Karen Nelson Bell, the Producer of Country Tonite Enterprises.

## About the Choreographer

John was nice enough to let me join him during a recent audition. The audition was held between shows and although he was pressed for time he gave me a little information about himself, the show and what he likes to see from the performer.

John Burdette grew up in a dance family. John's mother and father had a dance studio and were involved in putting together shows for many years. As he became a better dancer, it was a natural transition for him to start helping with choreography. It wasn't long before he just took over the entire responsibility. It's always better to work for someone who understands what dancers go through and what they need to excel. John is this type of choreographer. I saw him take time after the audition to tell each dancer individually what he thought they did well and what they should continue to work on. This type of feedback is extremely valuable because most of the time you never know what the choreographer thought of your work.

Country Tonite is in its fifth season in Branson Missouri and will continue into the foreseeable future. Which is nice if you're looking for a job with longevity. The shows are an hour and fifteen minutes long, with fast paced dance numbers and dancers backing singers. The show consists mostly of jazz dance but dancers are required to do some clogging. Now don't worry if you don't clog. John has taught many dancers to clog whether they had tap ability or not. In fact, he said sometimes it's easier to teach dancers without much tap training to clog.

The one thing he did stress is personality, so if you decide to audition make sure you bring yours with you. While I'm on the subject, let me relay something that happened at the audition. The dancers hit the stage to learn a clogging combination from the dance captain. John and I sat in the audience and we watched them dance. I could just imagine the dancers thinking, "I'll just learn this combination and then I'll really perform it later." WRONG. You are being evaluated while you're learning the dance, even while you're putting your tap shoes on. So, remember to smile and sell as much as you can from the time you enter the theater, until you get into your car. As I said this particular audition was held between regular performances. The stage was lit with only a rehearsal light. I could not believe that many dancers were dancing in the dark and only one dancer went out of her way to get into the light. Needless to say, the dancers in the light got all the attention. The dancers in the dark could have been smiling like crazy, but it was difficult to see them. Again at the end of the audition, John pointed out ways for the dancers to enhance their performing abilities, reduce their mistakes and develop their technique. He is a very professional and caring choreographer and I could tell the dancers appreciated that.

## About the Producer

Picture a producer in your mind for just a minute. Do you see some big cigar-smoking man sitting at a desk, talking on the phone? You know the minute you meet him, he knows nothing about dance, could care less about the art form and is only interested in making money. Who wants to work for someone like that? Well, you're in luck because Karen Nelson Bell is nothing like that. She knows plenty about the art form, loves dancers and I believe if she was able to, she would put on a leotard and tap shoes and dance right along side you. She is a producer that is interested in keeping dancers long-term. Karen and John want the audition process to be a positive experience and told me she is always trying to make the dancer feel comfortable so they can give their best audition. As I continue in the interview you will see that Karen, John and the rest of their team want a good cast, a happy cast and a show that will be successful for a very long time.

DM: *How long has "Country Tonite" been in Branson?*

KNB: "Country Tonite" is in its fifth season in Branson. We perform "Country Tonite" in a theater that Country Tonite Enterprises owns. We are into our second season in Pigeon Forge, TN., and we've done a few years in Las Vegas, so things are moving right along.

DM: *This is always a plus for the dancer when you know you are working for a producer that is established and not going to close the show and pull out with a two day notice.*

KNB: (Karen laughs)

DM: *Don't laugh, it happens. I hear that working in Branson is seasonal. Tell me about the season and how dancers cope with that.*

KNB: The season runs from March 7$^{th}$ to December 18$^{th}$. Now don't forget there's also a two-week rehearsal period before the season starts, so we're back together the last week of February. Some dancers love the time off. They save their money and go home to see family or friends, they go to New York and see a few shows, or they take another job for a couple of months. Others don't like the time off and they worry about money for the two-month period.

DM: *When you said seasonal, I was thinking more of a summer job but this is ten months out of the year. That's a pretty long season. Why does the show shut down for two months?*

KNB: Branson is beautifully set in the mountains and as you can imagine it is very tourist oriented. We have busloads of tourists coming from all over to see the shows. In the winter, the snow makes it difficult for the busses to come in, and without any tourists, there can be no shows. The busses are the lifelines in Branson.

DM: *I'm trying to get an image here. Are there really forty shows going on in this little town?*

KNB: I think there are forty-three theaters and I'm proud to say that "Country Tonite" was third last season in attendance.

DM: *Well, that's pretty good. How big is the cast?*

KNB: Thirty-three total and I think twelve are dancers.

DM: *I assume the dancers sign a contract for the entire season. Do they have to re-audition at the end of the contract in order to come back for the next year?*

KNB: No, I am hiring almost the entire cast back. Some dancers are moving on to other work but I like hiring everyone I can back for another season. It makes my job much easier. I know the dancers, they know the type of show we do and they know how to work and get the show done. We can also save time and money on costumes.

DM: *Tell me about the contract the dancers will sign.*

KNB: It's a very standard contract for the ten-month period. I don't believe in keeping prisoners. There is a two-week out clause if a dancer is unhappy or lands another job, as well as a two-week notice if, for some reason, their performance is not on par with the other cast members. I do try to add certain incentives for showing up every night and putting on a good performance. I've hired an excellent cast and I want that cast to be on stage. So if a dancer makes it through the entire season without a sick day they will receive five days additional compensation at the end of the contract.

If they miss one day, then they'll receive four days compensation at the end of the contract and so on. We've found this to be a good incentive for attendance and helpful to the dancer in December when they know they're going to have some time off.

DM:   *I know people are sensitive when discussing money, but tell me what you can about salary and benefits.*

KNB:  I'll tell you this. The salaries in Branson range from $400 to $800 a week and "Country Tonite" is towards the top end of that range. We are also very proud of benefits and the incentives we've put in this year. We have a bonus pool, where the cast will share in the profits "Country Tonite" takes in. They will receive a salary and a share in the profits at the end of the year. What this does is help us with marketing. If a dancer is in a restaurant and someone asks them what show they should see, they can recommend "Country Tonite" and help promote the show. It pays for them to be proud of and promote the show they're performing in.

DM:   *That's a great idea. What about other benefits?*

KNB:  We have a health plan where Country Tonite Enterprises will pay half the premiums and the dancers will pay the other half. This is brand new and I don't know of many shows anywhere offering this to the cast. We also have a 401K program where the Company will match investments the dancers make into their own retirement program. Again, this is unheard of in the industry and reinforces our philosophy of keeping a stable and solid cast.

DM:   *This is the type of information that needs to get to the dancer and to other types of employers, so they will also offer these benefits. I think every show that hires dancers should have a health plan and a retirement plan. Okay, tell me about the audition and how dancers can land this terrific job.*

KNB: John and I love dancers and we know how difficult the audition process can be. But first, let me tell you, we will usually place ads in local papers in different cities stating exactly what we're looking for. Because I also have the show in Las Vegas, I usually advertise in the Dirt Alert. The Dirt Alert is a great newspaper for performers looking for work all over the country and in many foreign countries. I will also place ads in dance studios, so it always pays to study. When you arrive at the audition you will be asked to fill out a sign-in sheet. This is not just name and address, it is a very in-depth sign-in sheet. John and I want to know as much about you as a person as we do about you as a performer. We enjoy the work we do and we want performers around us that feel the same way.

DM: *That makes sense. Now, what can the dancer do to really make an impression?*

KNB: Well, a couple of simple things. Show up on time, bring a picture and resumé and make sure they are stapled together. These things tend to get lost and it's important we have the right resumé with the right picture. From a performance point of view, "Country Tonite" is an all American, down home type of show. We are looking for expression and personality. We're looking for the kind of personality that travels across the footlights to the back of the theater. In this particular show, there are no masks or wigs and big headdresses. You are the show and you have to sell yourself. There is nothing to hide behind. We love vivacious and energetic performers of all races and nationalities. We encourage all races to audition but we are looking for a quality of wholesomeness. I know it's in style now to have tattoos and body piercings but that type of thing does not work for this show.

DM: *What about height and weight?*

KNB: Height is hardly ever a problem but we do try to keep everyone around the same height. There is never a height requirement but I have to tell you in all honesty, weight is something that many dancers have a problem with and weight is very important to me and to the production. If you are having a problem controlling your weight start working on it now.

DM: *What about dance? What will the audition consist of?*

KNB: Both the men and the women will do a jazz combination. This is a strong jazz combination and we like to see a good jazz background. We will also give a clogging combination. For those of you that know clogging, this is an Ozark style of clogging. It's important to know that each combination will be rated individually, so if your clogging is not real strong but your jazz is, we can evaluate that and teach you how to clog in the style we're looking for. We love acro – if you can perform some type of acrobatics, please be sure to let us know. And if you sing, there is sometimes room to move up into one of the principal roles. It doesn't happen very often but it has happened and it is an opportunity for advancement.

DM: *Thanks for all that information, but before I let you go, please tell me a little about the town of Branson.*

KNB: Branson is like stepping back in time. It's incredibly beautiful, the people are very friendly, and you don't have to lock your doors. A lot of dancers that have worked there have decided to stay. The first year, six dancers drove up from Florida and are still living here. It's hard to put into words other than "wholesome". I'm very happy to say that the cast is drug free, and this is not something I've had to worry about because the cast enforces the issue with their peers. It's just something that's not welcome here, on or off the stage.

DM: *Thanks again. I would like to give the dancers an address to submit pictures and resumés.*

KNB: Sure, they can send them to:

**Karen Nelson Bell**
101 S. Rainbow Blvd.
Suite 28-221
Las Vegas, NV 89121

## LEGENDS IN CONCERT

Before we discuss "Legends in Concert" I want to tell you about a very special choreographer, Bobby Boling. Bobby has done what every entertainment director, choreographer and teacher has told you to do, and that is, be versatile. Over the past two decades he has been a dancer, teacher, choreographer, director, lighting designer, writer, and composer. With that kind of versatility is it any wonder he's working all the time.

Have you noticed a theme throughout this book? The people that are successful in our business never stop learning. Bobby has taught dance in New York, Paris and Las Vegas. He has performed in all mediums and is the Artistic Director, Choreographer and Lighting Designer for On Stage Entertainment Inc. He has directed and choreographed all over the world including Las Vegas, Hawaii, Atlantic City, Lake Tahoe, Branson, Mo., Myrtle Beach, SC, Tokyo, Japan, Australia, China, Hong Kong, and Berlin. This is a choreographer you should know.

Fortunately, it's easy to find out what Bobby looks for in a dancer. He has an informative book out called "A Dancer's Manual". This is an exceptional guide on auditioning and preparing for a professional career in dance. We'll talk to him a little later but now, I want to take excerpts from his book so you can understand what Bobby Boling thinks about important dance topics.

### On Show Business

"I see so many dancers with so much talent, compassion, and love for dance. These dancers struggle because they are misinformed or worse, not informed at all. They don't know what is necessary for achieving success in show business."

"A good teacher is essential to a dancer's success in the entertainment industry."

"Yes, it's a freaky business but it's also exciting, challenging and rewarding. You can travel, meet many interesting people and get paid for it. It'll put a smile on your face and in your heart, because you're doing what you love to do."

### On Attitude

"A good attitude is the most important thing a dancer can have. I will always take a good dancer with a great attitude over a great dancer with a bad attitude."

"Attitude separates the real professionals from the pretenders."

"Don't beat yourself up about what you don't know or what jobs you didn't get. Every once in a while you have to give yourself credit for the things you do know and the progress you've made."

### On Preparation

"Take care of your body. While it's your mind that creates and stores technique, musicality, and expression. It's your body that enables you to communicate that knowledge and those feelings to your audience."

"Every dancer needs ballet! Ballet gives the dancer strength, control, line and the carriage a dancer needs to present themself in the most powerful and graceful way possible."

"Study! Read books, study films, go to shows and dance concerts, talk to choreographers, teachers and other dancers. Do whatever you can to learn the history of your profession but also keep up on what's happening in the business today."

"Technique, a good body, and a good look make up about fifty percent of what a professional dancer needs. The one quality that inevitably makes the difference between getting the job and going home, is how you communicate emotions and feelings through your dancing. The dancers that always seem to work have passion, excitement, confidence and style in their dancing."

**On Auditioning**

"If you know the combination very well, try to get downstage center. If you don't, stay in the back until you do."

"Ask questions, but be specific. Don't say, "I don't understand this part". It's always more impressive if you ask questions about style rather than steps. This tells the choreographer that you're willing to learn their style, a major compliment to any choreographer."

"Don't ever do more or less turns than the choreographer asks for. This alone tells the choreographer that you don't take direction very well."

"Have a sense of humor at the audition. Being able to smile and laugh conveys to the choreographer that you're fun to be around and that you handle pressure well."

"Sell, but don't oversell! I realize there's a fine line between doing it well and overdoing it, but smile because you enjoy it, not because you have this smile you pull out and paste on for auditions. Choreographers are looking for real people. Jaymi Marshall, a talented choreographer, always tells his dancers, 'Above all, be interesting.' I think that's perfect."

" 'You can't judge a book by its cover.' This expression doesn't work at the audition. You will be judged immediately on your looks. So ladies, dress clean and neat, wear make-up and style your hair. There is absolutely no excuse not to!"

Bobby had many other things to say on these topics but I don't want to give everything away. I want you read his book. It's just so much easier to audition for a choreographer when you know a little bit about their likes and dislikes. So, there's some inside stuff, now let's get to Legends in Concert.

DM: *Bobby, Legends in Concert is a great show that has been running for quite a while now. Tell me about the production company the dancer will be working for and the background on how the show got started?*

BB: Legends In Concert is just one of the productions produced by On Stage Entertainment Inc. Right now they have 14 full time productions. This is an entertainment company that has recently gone public and you can find them on the NASDAQ stock market. John Stuart started this show with a 3-week contract at the Imperial Palace and is now in its 15th season. The show is created around the best celebrity impersonators. When the show first started it had to be celebrities that were dead. In fact, John used to say that he would watch the obituary column to find out when he could use a new impersonator. The first show had four celebrity impersonations and now there are 115 different celebrities that have performed in Legends in Concert.

DM: *So at some point John decided to go with living celebrities also?*

BB:  Yes. There came a point when he realized he had to get the younger audience to come in and enjoy the show. That's when Elton John, Madonna, Whitney Houston and others started performing.

DM: *Let's get this out of the way.  The number one impersonation is?*

BB:  Without a doubt it's Elvis. John always said without Elvis there would have never been a show. I'll give you just a few of the names that are impersonated in Legends.  Elvis, Marilyn Monroe, Hank Williams, Elton John, Madonna, Whitney Houston, Barbara Streisand, Buddy Holly, Paul McCartney, Liberace, Kenny Rogers, Nat King Cole, Dolly Parton, Neil Diamond, and many more.  The thing that separates this show is the impersonators do their own singing and if the celebrity plays an instrument the performer plays that instrument also.  The performer playing Liberace actually plays the piano like Liberace.  Paul McCartney plays base and keyboards like Paul McCartney.  It's truly amazing! When someone comes in to audition for Whitney Houston you say to yourself, "Girl, you better really be able to sing because if you can't the whole audience will know."

DM: *Now, I know the Las Vegas show is the show that started it all but let's talk about Branson.  Are there differences between the two shows?*

BB:  Yes, the Las Vegas show is bigger than the Branson show.  The format is pretty much the same but as far as the dancers are concerned, in Branson there are four female dancers and two female singer dancers. In the bigger shows we add two male dancers.

DM: *What is the format?*

BB: There are usually seven acts, but some acts will perform two numbers. Elvis will perform 'Jailhouse Rock' and 'Viva Las Vegas.' Madonna might do 'Vogue' and 'Express Yourself.' The dancers will perform 10 to 12 dance numbers per show.

DM: *Always backing the star impersonator?*

BB: Yes.

DM: *When you change impersonators, the dancers will have to come in and rehearse new routines to back the new star?*

BB: Of course, they will learn the new numbers to back the new impersonator. The thing is, dancers that have worked the show for a couple of contracts, have a repertoire of 30 to 40 dance routines. Rehearsal for them is just a brush up to refresh their memory.

DM: *Oh, so the number you did for Elton John six months ago will be the same the next time an Elton John impersonator comes into the show?*

BB: I do make a few changes depending on the theater, but for the most part it will be the same.

DM: *I know Legends in Concert has been expanding to many cities. Tell the dancers reading this book where they're performing the show right now and where they'll be in the near future.*

BB: Right now we're in Las Vegas, Nevada, Atlantic City, New Jersey. Branson, Missouri, which you know is seasonal from March to December. Myrtle Beach, South Carolina, is also seasonal from March to December. We are in Berlin, Germany and will soon be in Cologne, Germany in September, 1998. We will open in Cancun, Mexico in May 1998 and the West End of London in October. We're in Honolulu, Hawaii, Lake Tahoe, Laughlin, and On Stage Entertainment recently purchased Wild Bill's in Orange County, California and that will soon be another Legends in Concert show. With the acquisition of Wild Bill's, there will be a few productions opening in Florida.

DM: *You are a busy man! Do you have a high turnover of dancers or do they stay for more than one contract?*

BB:   I'll tell you this, 80% of the dancers that have left the show to work somewhere else have returned to do another contract at some point. Most dancers stay for more than one contract and there are a few reasons for this. I know dancers, I like dancers and they're treated very fairly. Besides, the show is a lot of fun. The audience loves the show and we want the audiences to keep coming back, so we rotate the acts. This also makes it fun for the dancers because they're constantly doing new routines and not becoming bored. Another way I help the dancer is if they are in good standing, meaning easy to work with and professional, they can jump to another show after their contract is over. They may be in Atlantic City for six months and want to go to Cancun. After six months they might get tired of the beach and want to go to Germany. We can do that.

DM: *That sounds very exciting for a dancer. Let's talk about business. Evidently, they sign a six-month contract, what are the pay and benefits like?*

BB:   Yes, they sign a six-month contract. The dancers usually receive $600 to $650 a week. They have a medical and dental plan where On Stage Entertainment will pay half of the premiums and the dancer will pay half. Rehearsal pay varies quite a bit.

If you are a new dancer coming into the show, you may get $100 or so for the rehearsal week. If we're having a brush up rehearsal for a new number that's going into the show, it will probably pay $7.00 an hour. It varies from show to show so you should always ask.

DM: *I know that On Stage Entertainment has other shows they produce as well. Tell me about them.*

BB: I choreograph other productions for On Stage. We do magic shows, ice skating shows and right now I'm staging a show that is like Mystère on a smaller scale. We also do 20 to 40 corporate shows a year for companies like McDonalds, IBM, AT&T and many others. We do so many corporate shows that I have dancers that can almost make a living just doing that.

DM: *Great! How does a dancer contact you for an audition?*

BB: Each show is self-contained with its own company manager and dance captain. You can contact each theater individually or you can send a picture and resumé to:

On Stage Entertainment, Inc.
c/o John Stuart
4625 W. Nevso St.
Las Vegas, NV. 89103

We will also accept videotapes and have hired from tapes in the past.

While Bobby was staging his latest version of Legends in Concert in Branson, he interviewed a couple of dancers from the show. This way you could get information from the dancers that are actually living and working in Branson. I want Lisa Marie Moore and Kenya Caughy to get credit for helping dancers across the country discover the pros and cons of working in Branson.

Bobby:     Is there a season for Branson, and if so, what is it?

Dancers: There's definitely a season. It is from March though December. Most shows, as well as businesses, close for the months of January and February.

Bobby:     Do any shows stay open through January and February?

Dancers: Jim Stafford's show. That's about it.

Bobby:     What do the dancers do during those two months of down time?

Dancers: If they get a re-hire from their theater, they'll collect unemployment. Others will take side jobs in Springfield, MO (the nearest city), because even the waiter and waitressing jobs in Branson are dead. Some will teach at the local dance studio. Some will take other gigs.

Bobby:     Other gigs where?

Dancers: Well, last year, Florida was real popular. A lot of dancers got jobs there. Some tour with theater companies.

Bobby:     Would you say there is a big turnover of dancers in Branson?

Dancers: There's actually a lot of theater "hopping" in Branson. You'll know dancers that were in the Mel Tillis Theater, and all of a sudden, they're at the Showboat or at the Osmonds. Dancers can change shows often without ever having to leave Branson.

Bobby:     How do you find out about auditions? Is there a trade paper for entertainment?

Dancers: Unfortunately, there is no trade paper. Most auditions are advertised through word of mouth, and at the local studios. Some theaters will put an ad in the local newspapers in the entertainment section.  A lot of the bigger name theaters go to cities like Los Angeles, Las Vegas, and New York to audition.  Most of the time, it's through word of mouth.

Bobby:  You've mentioned dance studios.  How many are there in Branson?

Dancers: There are two of them.  Branson Performing Arts and Premier Dance Studio.

Bobby:  Do they offer classes for professionals and do they have good teachers?

Dancers: Yes, they offer classes in the morning before shows and usually the teachers are dancers from the shows but occasionally guest teachers will come through Branson.  Arthur Duncan is an example.

Bobby:  What would you estimate the average dancer salary to be in Branson?

Dancers Fifty dollars per show.  I'd say that a dancer could make anything from $450 to $800 per week in Branson.

Bobby:  Are any of the theaters in Branson union affiliated?

Dancers: No.  Missouri is a right-to-work state, so you don't need a union card to work here.

Bobby:  What's the cost of living like?  Is it cheap? Expensive?

Dancers: Not as cheap as people think.  It's because it's a tourist town and you have to take that into consideration.  But if you're coming from a big city, it is a lot cheaper to live here.

Bobby:  What would you guess the average monthly rent would be for an apartment in the area?

Dancers: I've paid anywhere from $450 to $675. You can get a nice two-bedroom apartment for between $600 and $650. However, know that during the down months (January and February), rates do go down and you can get apartments at a cheaper rate.

Bobby: What can you tell me about the weather in Branson?

Dancers: It's very pretty, and often very hot during the summer. But because Branson lies in the middle of the Ozark Mountains, it is not uncommon to get snowed or iced in during the winter months.

Bobby: I've been to Branson several times and I have never seen any form of public transportation. I take it that means you definitely need a car to live here.

Dancers: Most definitely! In fact, I've lived here for four years and just last week, I saw my first taxi. I'm sure it's the only one!

Bobby: What do you do for entertainment?

Dancers: Go to Springfield, St. Louis, or Kansas City. Otherwise, in Branson there are three health clubs and a lot of outlet shopping malls.

Bobby: What would you like to tell dancers that might be considering coming to Branson to work?

Dancers: I would say that you need to realize this town is built on family values. So, if you're coming from a big city, you might be in for somewhat of a culture shock. There's not a lot of nightlife here. There are a couple of nightclubs and a few restaurants and bars where the entertainers meet to socialize, but most are closed by midnight or one a.m. It's a little town with a lot of shows in it, but it's still a little town. I know many people who have come in and they either hate the place, or they really love it.  I guess it all depends on whether or not you like small towns.

# Chapter Seven

# Theme Parks

Although some major theme parks have closed, the big three – Disney, Universal Studios and Six Flags Over America are getting bigger and better all the time. I want to update both Disney and Universal Studios for you since they are both major employers for the dancer. I really wanted to include Opryland Theme Park in this chapter but you'll find out in the next chapter why that just didn't happen. Where most jobs we've talked about so far have undergone rapid changes it's kind of reassuring to note that theme parks pretty much stay the same. They continue to put a lot of dancers to work, creating new shows all the time, but their policies and their hiring practices remain the same. So let's discuss Disney and Universal Studios. The names are different, some of the shows are different but they're still fun places to make a living.

## UNIVERSAL STUDIOS

Universal Studios Theme Park is a major employer of dancers and an interesting job consideration. There have been a few changes at Universal Studios since the last edition of this book, but it remains a terrific opportunity for the dancer. Michael Laughlin has taken over the position of Talent Supervisor and has used his experience and expertise to create new shows and perfect the shows that have been running for a while. His self-description as a dancer "that's been around the block more than once" not only tells about his sense of humor but also conveys his experience as a performer and choreographer. Michael, like many dancers, has had the pleasure of dancing in almost every type of show from Broadway to dinner theater. Michael was extremely helpful in providing information and was excited to have this information passed on to you. Here is a list of shows running presently.

| | |
|---|---|
| *Beetlejuice* | *Land Before Time* |
| *Totally Nickelodeon* | *Doo wops* |
| *Blues Brothers* | *Wild West* |
| *Boom Operator* | *Waterworld* |

The Wild West and Waterworld shows are really stunt shows. A few dancers have been known to move into these shows because of their abilities but it's very rare.

Let me tell you a little bit about how Universal Studios works for the hired dancer. Universal utilizes a stepladder system. Each of the eight shows previously mentioned has 6 or 7 separate casts. When you're hired, you may be placed in cast 6 or cast 7 and as you train, perform and gain experience you'll move up to cast 1–3. This is very important since it is only casts number 1–3 that receive total health care benefits, not to mention priority with scheduling and vacations. This may initially sound harsh, but again it does encourage and reward long term employment.

Consider this! Universal Studios Theme Park will give a dancer time off to perform other jobs in the industry. This is unheard of in the dance world! It's called Professional Leave of Absence. Of course, the outside work must be approved by Universal and your time off is without pay, but your job will be secure until you return from your other dance job. This is great! While you're working at Universal you can audition for other dance jobs. Example... Say you land a job dancing on the Academy Awards Special. You'll be allowed to rehearse, perform the special, work for a new choreographer, make money, and gain experience... then return to a full time job right away. Michael Laughlin said, "We want a long term dancer, a happy dancer and an experienced dancer and we think it's important to allow a dancer to gain that experience and bring it back to Universal." This is a plus you can't put a monetary value on.

### About the Work

With many dance jobs you may work for a sub-contracted production company (see MGM Theme Park), but with Universal you become a Universal employee and receive the benefits that all Universal employees receive. Although park rules are standard for each show, contracts are different for each show. I wasn't able to see a contract so I can't help more than that, but I will say what I always say, READ IT!

One key benefit is insurance. After a three-month trial period, full insurance benefits including a dental plan are available for casts 1–3.

During the peak season (summer and Christmas) there is a five-day workweek and you are allowed to perform six

shows a day.  No one for any reason may perform more
than six shows in one day.  Every show is 10–20 minutes
of nonstop high energy dancing, singing and stunts.  Some
are heavily costumed or have heavy makeup and all of the
shows have pyro special effects.


## Pyro

You should remember that almost every show at
Universal has pyro effects.  Flash pot explosives and
firewalls all in close proximity to performers.  These
effects are wonderful for the audiences, but for the
dancers it's an extra hazard.  Stunt performers have
worked with pyro from the very beginning of their
careers, but dancers have not.  If I were performing in one
of these shows, I would pay very close attention during
rehearsals as to where and when these pyro effects are
going to happen.


## Money

Once hired you will enter into a rehearsal period of 2–
6 weeks depending on the show.  ASK!  Your rehearsal
pay is on an hourly wage, somewhere between $9 and $12
per hour, depending on the show.  You will also make an
hourly wage when you eventually train other casts.  You
see, casts 1–3 will train and clean up the performances of
casts 4–6.

Show pay is another story.  You are paid per show up
to six shows per day and the show pay varies greatly.  In
"Boom Operator" a dancer will make $16 per show and in
"Beetlejuice" a performer will make $38 per show.
Remember a show is 10–20 minutes long.

Lets use Beetlejuice as our example.  Show pay for
"Beetlejuice" is $38 per show.  During the peak summer
season "Beetlejuice" may be performed up to 15 times in
one day, as an example let's say you're in cast 3 and you

perform 5 shows from 3 P.M. to 8 P.M. That's $190 a day. Multiply that for a five day work week and an ambitious dancer can make a very nice salary. Including full medical and dental benefits, stable long term employment and the ability to perform industry jobs outside of the theme park and you have a place of employment few dance jobs can match.

I would like to give you a brief breakdown of each show, in case you'd like to submit a picture and resumé or call to find out when the next audition might be. So, let's begin with a show that's been running for a while and is still a crowd favorite.

## Beetlejuice

Beetlejuice has undergone a facelift and has moved indoors into its own theater. This show is heavily costumed with quite a bit of makeup. The lighting and pyro special effects are still terrific and work even better indoors. There are five dancers in the show and all dancers must sing. The 25-minute show is based on the movie with everyone singing rock songs. If you are going to audition for Beetlejuice, prepare a rock type audition piece and be prepared to dance both jazz and hip-hop. One thing Michael stressed, do not show up in costume! It is not needed and your interpretation of what Beetlejuice should look like might not be the same as Universal's interpretation. Just wear something to dance in and be prepared to sing.

## Totally Nickelodeon

This production is based on the television show and is geared towards a younger audience. There are two dance positions in this show and they perform four different numbers. The dancers must have jazz, tap and ballet training along with some street dance ability. The costuming is real casual, mostly overalls, and the dancers really have to interact with the crowd.  There are quite a few acting positions in this show.

If the dancers have the ability and show interest in playing one of the characters that is acceptable but the pay is the same for both actor and dancer.  The show is 25 minutes long and the pay for this production is $37.10 with a minimum of four shows per day.


## Blues Brothers

Dancers and characters for this show will have to sing and dance.  Michael has made a few changes with this particular show.  He removed a character that didn't make much sense and added a Cab Calloway character that fits perfectly.  The Blues Brothers used to perform on the street but have now moved onto their own Blues Brothers stage.  The Blues Brothers characters drive through the park in their old car from the movie and make their entrance.  Again the show is approximately 25 minutes long and it pays 32.90 per show.  Don't ask why it's $32.90 and not $33.  I think it's a rate increase that was negotiated based on percentages.


## Boom Operator

Boom Operator is a little bit different than most of the shows we've talked about so far.  First of all, it's only 10 minutes long and the pay is only $16 per show but you are guaranteed a minimum of 7 shows per day.  Okay, I'll do the math.  That's a minimum of $112 per day.  At the time of this writing the show is performed only on weekends but will go to full time shortly.  Boom Operator is a mini-version of "Stomp".  It's fun, contemporary and very funky so the three dancers performing this show will have to dance and have some percussion ability.  Michael did say that it has been taught to dancers that didn't have a percussion history before with few problems, especially if they have a strong tap background. Dancers with good tap training are used to picking up rhythms.

Universal Studios should be a consideration for any dancer in the business. Not only is it quality employment in and of itself but it's also a great stepping stone for dancers that come out to Los Angeles with the desire to dance in film and television. I have many friends that enjoyed their time performing at the theme park. The Universal theme park changes their production shows often, so call or write to get the latest shows being produced and how you can audition. The address is:

**Universal Studios Theme Park**
Entertainment Office
Universal City, CA  91610


# DISNEY

Disney is a major employer of dancers and is getting bigger all the time. I spoke with John Anello, Manager of Talent Resources for the West Coast. Ronny Rodrigues is casting manager for the Florida properties. Because LA is so large with an enormous pool of dancers, John will cast almost exclusively in LA. Ronny Rodrigues will cast in Florida, but mostly travels around the country in search of dancers, dancer–singers, singers and masters of ceremony.

John gave me a few examples of how dancers are utilized in all Disney properties. Parade dancers; dancers and characters hired for specialty parades. Special productions; shows like "Animazement", that will have limited runs. Finally, as an example, shows like "Golden Horseshoe" that are staples of the park and will most likely run forever. Disney is very protective of their image. Getting information from Disney was difficult and they remain vague on a variety of topics but here's what they did say.

DM: *I don't think dancers are aware of how many dancers Disney hires.*

JA:   That may be true.  It's an interesting thing.  We advertise in all LA trade papers and Ronny will tour the country to cast for the three Florida properties.

DM: *What are some of the differences?*

JA:   Well, I really can't speak for Ronny, but because they bring people to Florida from other areas, they usually have a year contract.  In LA, I do a lot more short-term projects and one shot deals, except for our stage productions.

DM: *I remember shows like the "Golden Horseshoe" using dancers.*

JA:   Right!   "Golden Horseshoe" in LA, "Diamond Horseshoe" in Florida.   In those shows we have horseshoe dancers, can–can dancers and the guy dancers are cowboys.   This is a long-term production.

DM: *Different for parade dancers?*

JA:   Yes, parade dancers are a whole different level of dancer and fill a different requirement.  I don't hire parade dancers, that's another department.  But very often a parade dancer that has been with us awhile will move up into one of our productions.

DM: *Tell me about the production shows.*

JA:   The ongoing shows like the "Golden Horseshoe" run five days a week.

DM: *More in the summer?*

JA:   No, probably not.  I think it will remain five days a week, five shows a day, as of right now.  The show we're running presently at Videopolis is "Animaze-ment the Musical". It opened in June and will probably run for a year. We've been running only weekends, but recently went to seven days. We'll keep it seven days a week through the summer. At this point, we don't know if we'll continue with "Animazement the Musical" or not, so neither do the dancers. That's one of the problems with limited runs.

DM: *How many dancers are in "Animazement the Musical"?*

JA: Approximately 8–10 dancers in the show plus substitutes in case someone is sick or hurt.

DM: *A big production. Are the dancers costumed as characters, or is my image wrong?*

JA: Very rarely, the dancers are in crowd scenes as townspeople or ballroom couples. They are the glue that moves the show along. It's a mix. Many of our shows are a mix of dancers, characters and principal roles.

DM: *How long is the show?*

JA: Our shows are 25 minutes.

DM: *Will they sing?*

JA: When we audition, we'll almost always ask dancers to sing. In this particular show they'll just dance.

DM: *What will a dancer make for this type of show?*

JA: I can't tell you that.

DM: *All right then. Tell me what you look for in a dancer.*

JA: When we did "Animazement the Musical" some of the dancers had to have strong ballet training, others had to have a strong tap and jazz background. The advice we give to people is they need to do it all.

They should constantly be in dance class. The frustration we have in casting is that many times a dancer has a certain strength in one area, but not in another. What makes a dancer valuable to us is versatility. For our purposes, the choreographer needs to feel no matter what they come up with to make a show work, the people they've hired will be able to pull it off. A dancer's strength is versatility.

DM: *What's the rehearsal period?*

JD: Well, generally speaking a rehearsal period is two to three weeks. Rehearsals will be local or at the park.

DM: *I know you can't give me figures, but rehearsal pay is different from show pay?*

JA: Yes. If you contact AGVA (The American Guild of Variety Artists) you can find out what the going rates are.

DM: *Then Disney follows AGVA minimums?*

JA: Well, every park cuts their own deals. I'm just in no position to talk money. All I can say is there's a rate for rehearsals and a rate for performance.

DM: *Are the dancers hired by Disney – employees of Disney – or are they sometimes hired by a production company?*

JA: Dancers working in the park will be Disney employees while they are working. We don't sub-contract shows to independent production companies in the park.

DM: *What about shows that tour, like "Hercules" and "Pocahontas"?*

JA: The hiring process may be different. If they've hired outside the park it may not always be AGVA.

DM: *What about benefits?*

JA: Depends on time worked. You have to have a certain number of hours per week and a certain number of weeks worked. There are all kinds of levels. They have numbers like 02, 03. Depending on time, each one of those levels dictates the amount of coverage they get.

DM: *So a dancer is rewarded for long term employment?*

JA: Yes. The dancers at the "Horseshoe" tend to be involved longer than "Animazement the Musical" and other shows. They would accumulate benefits.

DM: *Any type of height requirements or ethnic background.*

JA: No, never, if they're good, they're good! We hire everybody.

DM: *Anything else about the audition process you'd like to see.*

JA: I like to see a dancer come prepared. If you are asked to sing, bring an up–tempo and a ballad. Dress comfortably, but dress so it shows you at your best. We will set up the audition out of this office. A choreographer, show director, my casting assistant and myself will hold the call. The thing dancers must know – they get one shot to show what they can do. They should take inventory of themselves. Be smart! Be realistic, and say, "What is it I can show these people, that will make them feel they need to have me in their show." Studying, practicing and being prepared! You need to tell them to continually take dance class. They better start learning to sing also because more and more we need both. When we hire, the difference between the one we hire and the one we didn't may be their ability to sing.

DM: *What about picture and resumé?*

JA:   They should <u>always</u> have a good, current picture and resumé. We do consider it because we want to see their experience. That doesn't mean if they don't have experience they won't be hired. We just hired a girl fresh out of school. It just happened that she came in and blew us away. She was well trained and well prepared.

DM: *Do you hire in LA for parks in Paris and Japan?*

JA:   Actually, there's a tour that goes around the country every six months to find talent for Japan. Ronny Rodrigues does that tour with a choreographer and a show director from Japan. They make the decisions and we make all the job offers from this office.

John Anello was very helpful in letting us know what Disney's needs are in terms of dance. John Anello is retiring soon and I want to wish him the best of luck.

Disney is a little secretive in terms of money, but that's their prerogative. Not everyone is comfortable talking about money. I did contact AGVA. They told me they do have contracts with Disney. In fact, they have contracts with Universal and Six Flags. Disney does adhere to AGVA minimums in the theme park.

I can't tell you exactly what you'll make working the "Golden Horseshoe" but AGVA minimums are $670 per five day week for dancers and $793 per five day week for principal roles. AGVA also has medical benefits for dancers after a certain amount of work is performed. At Disney, this period is 15 days in one show. After 15 days, Disney will begin to contribute to your insurance premiums. This changes frequently from park to park. Universal, on the other hand, begins paying into your benefits after six months!

Disney should be considered as a good and major employer of dancers. You can stay in one park or tour. You can have long term employment or audition for a limited run.    Many dancers in LA work Disney and audition for other jobs.    So take John's advice.    Be prepared and give it your best shot.    Watch for audition notices in trades or your local newspaper.    For more information you can call the Disney Hotline number in Anaheim at 714-781-0111 and in Florida, 407-397-3220. If you'd like to submit to Disneyland, send a picture and a resumé to:

**Talent Booking**
Disney Entertainment
P.O. Box 3232
Anaheim, CA  92803

# Chapter Eight

# Production Companies

Production companies are a mysterious part of our business. Many dancers don't understand who they are and what they do. I told you about a few quality production companies in the original "Dancing... For A Living" and I think the topic is so important, I want to expand on it.

Let's use Six Flags Over America as a hypothetical example. Six Flags is a major theme park with ten different parks across the country. Major cities like Atlanta, Dallas, Los Angeles, San Jose and others have their own Six Flags. Six Flags will produce, choreograph and design their own productions, but they can't produce all of their entertainment, so, often they will sub-contract a show to a production company.

What this means is, production companies from around the country will contact Six Flags and pitch their ideas for a show in the park. They will have meetings to discuss ideas, costumes, music, lighting and most importantly, budget. Six Flags will decide which production company came in with the best idea, and give that production company a contract to produce the show for them. This production company will then create the show from start to finish.

I'm telling you this because dancers auditioning for Six Flags, assume they will be a Six Flags employee. The truth is, they are often an employee of the production company that has the contract. Try to follow this a little further. Let's say I own Sunset Productions. Six Flags liked my idea for a show and gave me a budget of $400,000 to create this show from top to bottom. If I can put this show together for $200,000, guess who gets to keep the rest of the money? That's right, me. Now, of course, everyone is in the business to make money. You should be too! But as you can see, the situation can be very tempting for Sunset Productions to try to cut corners and make as much money as they can.

Let's say that I am a very greedy producer. (I know it's hard to believe, but let's say it's true.) I want Six Flags to be happy with the show I produce, so it's hard to scrimp on costumes and lighting because I want the show to look good. I may, however, be able to pay the dancers a little less money per week. I might not want to offer health benefits or a retirement plan because that would cut into my profits. I might hire non-union, inexperienced stagehands to work the show backstage. This can make the backstage environment a little more dangerous for the dancer. I might ask the dancers that really want the job to rehearse for free or offer a featured position for no extra salary. I know that dancers really want to dance and I can take advantage of that. Remember, I'm just a good businessman. I want you to know that there are many production companies like Sunset Productions out there.

So why am I telling you all this terrible information before I talk about quality production companies? I'll tell you a little story to make the point. A friend of mine is a bank teller and she handles money all day long. One day I asked her, "How did they train you to detect counterfeit money? Did they show you hundreds of different counterfeit bills so you could see all the fakes that are out there?" She said, "No, they let you handle real money, day in and day out. If you are constantly involved with the real thing, you can spot a counterfeit immediately." That is what I'm trying to do in this chapter. If I keep telling you about quality, reputable production companies and what they have to offer the dancer, then you will spot a shady production company immediately.

Earlier we talked with "Country Tonite Enterprises" and "On Stage Entertainment Inc," two quality production companies. Let me give you another example of a well-established hard working production company where you might seek employment.

## OPRYLAND PRODUCTIONS

When I first wrote Dancing...For A Living I wanted to talk with Opryland Productions about Opryland Theme Park. In the first book I covered Disneyland, Universal Theme Park and Six Flags over America. I didn't have the time or the money to cover Opryland, so I made it a priority in this revised edition to get the information to you. I spoke with John Heywood, executive director of Opryland Productions. As luck would have it, Opryland Theme Park has now closed it's doors, but the more I spoke with John, the more I realized there was a lot of information here that every dancer should be interested in. Sometimes, life closes one door only to open another, and that was the case with Opryland Productions.

Opryland Productions is a subsidiary of Gaylord Entertainment Company. Gaylord Entertainment has been in the entertainment industry for over 70 years and is listed on the New York Stock Exchange.

Okay, time out for one second. I'm not telling you these things because I'm doing some public relations work for Gaylord Entertainment. I'm telling you this so you can see that Opryland Productions is stable, well established and has a history of working with entertainers. There are a lot of fly-by-night production companies out there. I don't want you to find yourself in a situation where the show closes, the production company is gone and they've taken your last check. In that situation, (and it still happens) you have very little recourse. With Opryland Productions not only is that not going to happen but if something like that did, Gaylord Entertainment would be very easy to find. Okay, having said that, let's be more positive.

Opryland Productions is an entertainment production company specializing in producing spectacular events and quality theatrical presentations worldwide. They create all types of shows including trade shows, touring shows, theater, half-time shows for college bowl games, stage shows, casino shows, video productions and background entertainment. I know I told you Opryland Theme Park just closed but Opryland Productions still produces shows for the Opryland Hotel, The Grand Ole Opry, The Ryman Auditorium, The Governors Palace in Pigeon Forge, TN., Celebrity Cruise Lines, the Alabama Theater and the Wildhorse Saloon. This production company will produce almost 1500 different productions this year alone and that is why you need to know them. I will briefly tell you about a few upcoming productions and I'll tell you about what John Heywood likes to see when he auditions dancers.

## The Governor's Palace, Pigeon Forge, TN

Pigeon Forge is about 170 miles northeast of Nashville and is rumored to be the next Branson, Missouri. It doesn't have as many theaters as Branson yet, but it is growing very rapidly and I wouldn't be surprised to see thirty to forty theater productions there in the next five years. Opryland Productions will be opening their review on August 1$^{st}$ 1998 and the show will have a cast of 36 with 16 full time dancers. Like Branson Missouri, Pigeon Forge will have seasonal employment. The season will begin in April and end in December. Many of the particulars haven't been worked out yet because at the time of this writing the show isn't in rehearsal and the cast hasn't been hired yet. I just want you to know where dance jobs will be available in the coming years.

## Celebrity Cruise Lines

Opryland Productions is responsible and contracted for producing six different shows on two separate ships for Celebrity Cruise Lines. Royal Caribbean Cruise Lines owns Celebrity Cruise Lines. This is important because the cruise line industry is consolidating and changes happen very rapidly. Again, I will give you the highlights of working on Celebrity Cruise Lines and you can decide if this might be the job for you.

Most of the cruises will be one-week excursions through the Caribbean but there is also a cruise that will take you through the Panama Canal and up to Alaska. An exceptional cruise if you can get it! You will perform three different reviews during the week. Each review will be shown three times during the course of the evening. It's really simple math, the showroom holds 1,000 people and the ship has 3,000 passengers, so in order for everyone to see each production, you have to perform the show three times per night. But think about it for a minute, if you leave on Sunday and you return to port on Sunday, and you're only working three nights out of the week. That's not a tough schedule.

There is a work duty, though, and I will tell you about that later. You will share a crew cabin and you will eat with the crew, unlike some other cruise lines where you eat with the passengers. Although I've been told the food is good, this is still something to consider. The salary is

$500-$800 per week depending on your role in the show and rehearsal pay will be half your weekly salary. If you're replacing a dancer in mid-contract then you will rehearse on board ship. If it's the start of a new contract, then you will rehearse in Nashville. The contracts are six months in length and there is an option to renew, but as John Heywood and many others have told me, six months on a cruise ship is usually enough at one time. Many dancers have done a contract, gone on to do other work and returned to the ship a few years later, but to do more than one contract at a time is rough. You will enjoy the islands and many people have a great time aboard ship but the isolation can start to get to you. It's very difficult to take class and almost impossible to land your next job from the ship.

The theater on board ship is state-of-the-art. Although they have to be creative with limited backstage storage space, there is good fly space for sets, an orchestra pit and quality lighting.

## Work Duty

In your contract with Celebrity Cruise Lines, Royal Viking Lines or any other cruise line, you may be obligated to perform a work duty besides your show performance. Read it carefully! These duty obligations are different from ship to ship. Some cruise lines don't schedule work duty for dancers. Others don't have work duty for principals, just chorus. Here are a few things you should know about work duty:

1. The Cruise Director is ultimately in charge of work duty although the line captain from the cast may designate specific jobs.

2. Work duty is usually a sport, game or event. You will help coordinate the event; e.g. Ping-Pong Tournament or Water Volleyball.

3. Your one work duty per day will be no longer than two hours and not later than noon on show days. This is in your contract! Some Cruise Directors will try to take advantage of the situation and get you to work longer. Remember, you don't have to if you don't want to. This brings me to my next point.

4. I've had friends who've gotten restless on a cruise ship after 3 or 4 months and wanted to work other duty events. If you want to work more than one duty event, you can, but don't let your performance suffer.

5. For more information on cruise lines see the chapter on Disney Cruise Lines.

## Questions to Ask

Whatever cruise line you're considering, the answers to the following questions are a <u>must</u>:

1. Salary
2. Rehearsal Pay and Per Diem
3. Work Duty
4. Living Arrangements
5. Eating Arrangements

I've highlighted just a few of the opportunities Opryland Productions has to offer. Remember, I said they produce over 1,500 shows a year. Well, how can that be possible? Opryland Productions is involved with hundreds of industrial shows and trade shows each and every year. For those of you that have never been involved with trade shows, let me tell you first hand that they may not always be the most creative shows you'll ever be involved with but they can be very lucrative.

## Industrials

Trade and industrial shows are shows involving a sponsor or corporation that wants to use entertainment to promote a new product line or introduce a new aspect of their company. The balance of entertainment and the presentation of technical material make the show a delight to watch. It is far more effective in getting the new information to employees or distributors, than a long speech at a business meeting. These corporations will spend a lot of money to introduce a new product line at a trade show. John has informed me of budgets upwards of a million dollars. Let me give you an example of how this works, how the Production Company earns their money and how the dancer fits into the whole concept.

Let's say Honda is coming out with a new prototype automobile and they want to present it at a national convention. At this convention, all the Honda Dealers from around the world will come to see the latest product line Honda is creating. John Heywood and Opryland Productions will get together with executives from Honda and discuss budget, size and scope of the show, and if there's a slogan or a theme to the show. Very often, Opryland Productions will have to create a slogan or a theme to the show and then incorporate the dancers and singers to fit that theme.

Here's an example. The Honda show was going to be held at Harrahs. Harrahs is a major hotel/casino in Reno, Nevada. It just so happens that the owner of Harrahs has an amazing antique car collection and Opryland Production received permission to use these fine automobiles in the Honda trade show. Opryland Productions came up with the idea of building a musical show around the history of the automobile, culminating with the introduction of Honda's new prototype vehicle. Sounds great, doesn't it? Well, Honda loved the idea and the show was put into motion. The dancers and singers may do a Charleston number around a 1929 Oldsmobile or a number from "Grease" next to a 57 Chevy. You can start to see all the possibilities John Heywood might be able to use.

But this type of show is not without risk and that risk includes the dancer. Unlike a review or theater show where you'll get to perform a six month run, an industrial show like this one will be done one time, for a large audience. The dancer doesn't get a second chance and has to be perfect opening night. You will probably rehearse a week to ten days and get to perform this show once and go on to your next job. As you can imagine, Honda will be very meticulous about every aspect of the show and there will be a lot of tension and stress on the stage. They have millions and millions of dollars riding on a terrific presentation.

This Honda trade show went perfectly for the dancers, John, and Opryland Productions, but John shared a story with me about an industrial show that didn't go so well. Once again, Honda was introducing their new car and the moment of truth was about to take place on the stage. The car was beautiful and every single piece of the car was taken apart, cleaned, polished and detailed in every way possible. A special detailing company was hired to make the car shine like no other. They spent four days cleaning the car and putting it all back together. Honda spent thousands of dollars on hydraulic lifts so the car could be suspended in air and tilted in every conceivable position. So, the music soared, the smoke machine was covering the stage with fog and the curtain was slowly rising. The audience was getting their first glimpse of Honda's proud new automobile and although the car was beautiful and shining like the sun, a detailer forgot to connect one of the headlights back after polishing it. So, this beautiful vehicle was floating in mid-air with one headlight out. Honda was not happy and the detailing company lost a very large contract.

The point of telling you this is to let you know about the work you may be accepting. Industrial shows can be one day or they may be a weeklong and you might perform multiple shows. The good side to work like this is that it usually pays very well – sometimes two to three thousand a week for shows like the famous Pontiac industrials. But there will be a lot of stress on the set. To use our example story, Honda is under a lot of pressure to make sure the show is perfect. The production company will want to keep this account. The choreographer will want to have a good showcase for the production company and this will all filter down to you. Everyone will demand the absolute best you can give. I know this is not a problem since most dancers always want to give their best, but I want you to know what is expected of you in every aspect of the dance industry.

I've always enjoyed industrial work and continue to do it today. I've performed as a model, as a dancer, and today, as a spokesperson. I like learning about the computer industry or the electronics industry. I've done industrials from ski shows to pizza shows, (yes, they have conventions about pizza!)

I was once involved in a show for a power equipment company. We demonstrated everything from outboard motors, to lawnmowers, to chainsaws. I was hired as one of four presenters, but one presenter was the lead and the three of us would come on stage to present our smaller sections. I was hired by a very large and respected production company and was working for a choreographer who is an old friend and is unbelievably talented. The lead presenter forgot his lines and stood on the stage for thirty seconds not being able to recover. If you've ever been on stage, you know that thirty seconds is a lifetime when you can't remember a dance step or your next line. By the time we went out to rescue him it was far too late. The production company lost the contract and my choreographer friend was fired and blamed for not preparing the talent well enough.  It had nothing to do with preparation but when the client is not happy in this particular field of entertainment, everyone takes the blame.

Let's look at all the positives in performing this type of work.  As I said earlier, industrials usually pay well.  Many industrials are union and will pay Equity or AFTRA scale.  Industrials are almost always short term and you won't be away from home very long.  In my case, I love to do regional theater, but doing regional theater keeps me out of Los Angeles for six to eight weeks at a time.  I end up missing out on a lot of film and television auditions.  With an industrial, I can make the same money in five days that I can in a six week run doing a play.  Even though I may enjoy doing the play more, doing an industrial may be a smarter career move.  Another positive is travel.  You may get to perform all over the world as a dancer doing industrials.  Germany and Australia are two countries that have very large conventions and like to use dance to promote industry.  Pay, travel, short term and variety are just a few of the benefits to doing industrial work.

Opryland Productions has so much going for it in the variety of employment they have to offer.  Stage shows, cruise lines, and industrials are just a few examples of the dance work you may be involved in if you're fortunate enough to be hired by this company.  Now, let's find out what John likes to see in a dancer he hires and how we can get you an audition.

DM: *John, this book tries to inform dancers of quality work.  Sometimes this work is non-union but it is still quality work.  How would you sum up the type of work you offer dancers?*

JH:  There is something I want to mention right away.  I've been doing this for twenty-five years now and I want to stress to the dancer that not only are we offering good opportunities, but the level of talent, discipline and professionalism that these jobs require is really a good training ground for other types of work. We have had a ton of dancers and singers leave here and go on to Broadway shows. What use to be a credit on your resumé that carried very little weight, now carries a lot of weight, because of the number of people we have on Broadway. Broadway knows the quality of shows that we do. It's been very rewarding for me to hear dancers thank us for the training, professionalism and the experience they got by doing our shows.

DM: *What would you consider the dancers' most important attribute to be?*

JH: Well, of course training, but I really feel for our special need, I like to see versatility. We have shows where we have clogging, singing, and acrobats that need to do backhand springs and full twists and things like that. We are always looking for a variety of talents, so versatility is real important.

DM: *Is there room for advancement, and can a dancer go from one show to a better paying show?*

JH: Of course. Not only can they go to a better paying show, but we encourage it. If they have been doing a show for a period of time, we want them to go to a new show to become creative and fresh. In fact, after they have been an employee for two or three years we encourage them to go on to Broadway or whatever the next step might be for them.

DM: *All right, let's talk about how a dancer can get a job and work for Opryland Productions. I know you audition around the country in major cities, but can a dancer submit a picture, resumé and possibly a dance tape and get hired?*

JH: Absolutely. You know if you had asked me that four or five years ago I would have said, "No, you have to come to the audition." Now with good dance demo tapes and the fact that we need dancers all the time, you can submit and be hired. Remember, we do a lot of conventions and industrials and this type of work pays well, but may only work for a week or two. The thing about convention work is we might need a dancer that can also skate, or juggle, or walk on stilts or do a stage fight. So we will keep your tape on file and may call you for a special event. Many dancers have done a few conventions for us, and we really enjoyed working with them so, we offered them longer-term employment. You never know.

DM: *Great! Where would you like that tape and picture sent?*

JH:  Send it to:
**Opryland Productions**
2802 Opryland Dr.
Nashville, TN 37214

DM: *Back to the audition. When you tour, you place ads in major newspapers. Are your ads specific regarding what you're looking for?*

JH:  No, so don't be misled. We have so many shows going on at one time, we wouldn't have room to put in everything we're looking for. I may need a tap dancer for a particular convention and, in this instance, it doesn't matter if they have any ballet or singing experience. Now that's rare but, again, there is so much going on that anyone interested in working should come to the audition.

DM: *Will all dancers have to sing at the audition.*

JH:  Yes, and there are a lot of reasons for this. One, it tells you an awful lot about attitude just to have them come out, present themselves and do a song. Two, is I've heard dancers say "Oh well I can't really sing." And you'd be surprised! I'll give you an example. Cynthia Rhodes who was in "Dirty Dancing" and "Flashdance", she started with us and thought she couldn't sing. After working at it a while she went on to be a singer in a band. So don't put yourself down, just give it a try.

DM: *I have often heard Producers stress attitude, attitude, attitude. How does attitude come into play with your production company?*

JH:  Dancers should know that I watch their attitude from the moment they come in the door. How they relate to the other dancers. How they approach their craft. They can have a terrific talent, but if they don't work well with others, it's just not worth it. I'll tell you where attitude carries the most weight. It's when you have two dancers that are pretty equal in talent but you can only take one. You are going to take the dancer with the best attitude. It's as simple as that. Of course, I watch how they dance, but more importantly I watch how they pay attention when things are explained to them. I watch how pleasant they are at the call and how well they did the things you asked them to do.

DM: *If you would, give me a range of what a dancer can expect to make.*

JH:  Again, there are so many shows and it varies depending on the show and versatility of the dancer, i.e. if they're a dance captain or swing dancer, but I would say our dancers make anywhere from $450 to $1000 a week.

I want to thank John Heywood for his expertise and for sharing this information with the dancer. There are a few highlights I want to reiterate if you are considering auditioning for Opryland Productions.

1. This is a first class organization that has been working with entertainers for a long time. They

are conscious of dancers' needs and understand that dancers are athletes – physically and professionally.

2.  They are doing hundreds and hundreds of shows per year. If you are a college student this could be a great summer job. Get your stage time, make some money, and have some fun all at the same time. It may help you decide if a dance career is for you. Other dancers may just want to go on file and do special events. This can work too. If you're only available part of the year, you may pick up an extra show or two freelancing with Opryland Productions. Another plus is you may be able to transfer to The Alabama Theater or to a cruise ship. It's always nice to go from one job directly to a new one.

3.  Nashville. Some dancers don't take well to New York or LA and want a little different lifestyle. Well, Nashville might be just the place for you to enjoy life and still make a living doing your life long dream. I have only been to Nashville a couple of times but I've always enjoyed myself. The people, the music, and the hospitality are just what you might expect. Anyway you look at it, Opryland Productions is a company that needs to know who you are. Submit your information to them. You never know what can happen.

## Chapter Nine

# Regional and Dinner Theater

I'm going to take a different approach in this chapter. I will tell you about working in the theater and introduce you to an established director/choreographer. But the point I want to emphasize is that every dancer must do theater. You have heard Patsy Swayze recommend acting and voice to dancers and you've heard choreographers like Jerry Jackson demand emotion from the dancers he hires. I was watching a performance by the American Ballet Theater and was spellbound by the acting. I expected to be impressed with the dance by I didn't expect to be blown over by the emotion. Acting is essential to your longevity in dance.

I started in musical theater as an actor. We were doing South Pacific in a very nice dinner theater in Central Florida. In the chorus was a group of dancers that dared me to come to dance class with them. I was nineteen at the time and unafraid of anything. I had so much fun in dance class, I made it a daily event but I also kept up my acting training. It still amazes me that very few dancers take acting class and voice class. The day of the dancer making a living with dance alone is gone and nothing will improve your performance and your value to an employer like acting. You don't have to be Meryl

Streep but you have to have an understanding of the craft. Acting is like any other art form, it must be studied. You wouldn't expect to pick up a violin and be able to play it but people think because they can talk, they can act. It's just not true.

I was a very average dancer. I started dancing very late in life but I had a few things going for me. I'm over 6'2" tall and I had acting experience. When I auditioned for "A Chorus Line" the audition was very similar to the actual show. The first day, they gave us a ballet and jazz combination and then they made a cut. The second day, we did a tap combination, sang our audition song and then they cut again. The third day, there were only ten dancers left from well over two hundred and we were handed scenes from the script. I couldn't believe how nervous the remaining dancers were. I was finally comfortable with the audition because I knew I could act but none of the other dancers had a method they could rely on. They hadn't studied acting and they didn't know what to do.

I know it's difficult for many of you to take dance, acting and singing. I know a lot of dance studios don't offer all three classes at their studios, so I'm going to make this challenge to you. I challenge you to get into a play. If you're in high school get into a high school production. They love to use dancers and maybe you will get a few lines to read. If you're not in school, find a Dinner Theater in your area or try Community Theater. Most Community Theater productions don't pay a salary, but then again you won't have to pay them for the lessons you will learn. In musical theater almost everyone will sing, dance and act. You will work with a musical director and you will sing at every rehearsal. This alone can build your vocal muscles and give you more confidence. You may be lucky enough to say a line or two in the play but the important part is you'll get to work with a director and you will get to watch how actors work. You can learn so

much from watching quality people perform that sometimes this is more helpful than taking a class.

You've heard many choreographers and producers talk
about versatility and how important it is to them. The
theater is where you can learn to become versatile and
more valuable as a performer.

### Interview With Rob Barron

I want you to meet another dancer. He is much like
the others I've interviewed in that he wouldn't take no for
an answer and continued to climb from dance to
choreography to directing. He was lucky enough to know
at a very young age that he wanted to perform and he was
smart enough to study everything he could about dance,
voice and acting. Rob Barron has performed in over
twenty different musicals. He has directed and
choreographed forty other musical productions. He is in
constant demand as a choreographer and he told me he
enjoys every minute of it. I asked him a few questions
about Dinner Theater, Regional Theater and Equity
Theater.

DM: *Rob, please help me explain to dancers why it is so
beneficial for them to do theater.*

RB:  First, it's a way of learning your craft. This is a
never-ending process. You must continue to strive
to get better and better. Second, you get an
opportunity to work with a variety of directors –
some good ones and some bad ones. It's funny, but
you will learn from both. Another thing that is very
important is that it will keep you in front of your
public. I call it "stage time". Everyone needs stage
time and your public will always tell you how you're
doing. You must listen to them. If your timing is
off, they will tell you. Just like they will tell you if
they loved a dance number. If you have a line that is

supposed to get a laugh and you're not getting the laugh, you have to make the adjustment. You must listen to them, that's how you learn. This type of feedback can't be taught in class, you learn it on the stage. Dancers should do dinner and regional theater work any time they can get it.

DM: *Tell us about the selection process. How do you cast for a theatrical production?*

RB:  Well, I do have to start with type. If I'm doing a show that Ethel Merman originated on Broadway, then of course, I'm going to start there. I'm going to look for a strong belting voice that's brassy and bold. The dancer should know that my mind could be changed if you come in and knock my socks off. That's why it's so important to be yourself and don't try to just imitate because sometimes casting will change in a minute.

I'll give you an example of what I'm talking about. I was casting a television commercial. We were searching high and low for a dark haired little girl to play in this commercial. Why she had to have dark hair, I don't know, that's what the producers wanted. It was a commercial for Yellow Pages and they just had to have a young girl with dark hair. At the end of the day, this little dark haired boy sticks his head in the door and says, "Hey you guys, my mom wants to know if my sister is done yet." Well, the producers loved the energy of this little boy and everything changed on the spot. It is so important to be yourself because very often what happens is, if you do a great job, we will think of you for another role or part in the show.

Dancers should familiarize themselves with the show and with the character. If it's a show you are not familiar with, go to the library and get the play. Very often, you can listen to the soundtrack and get the feel of the music. Then when you come in to audition, you will sing something appropriate. You don't have to sing a song from the show but you should sing a tune that is close to that era. If you are going to audition for "Grease" don't sing a song from the "20's". If you're going to audition for "Rent" don't do a song from "La Traviata". It's just basic common sense. If you're going to do a rock musical, bring in a rock song. If you're auditioning for "Showboat", don't you dare bring in a rock song. I've seen this so many times from inexperienced dancers.

DM: *When they come to the call, how should they look? (i.e. shoes, clothes, hair)*

RB: Please bring all that, shoes, clothes and of course, hair. No really, be prepared for anything. Bring dance clothes even though you may wear street clothes into the call, especially if you were told you were going to sing first. Bring all shoes, tap, jazz and heels.

And look good! There is a performer in town and she's a wonderful dancer and beautiful soprano but she comes in looking like a scrubwoman. I know what she can do but the producers don't know what she can do and I have to fight to get her a job in my show. You don't have to come into an audition in costume but give me a little essence of what the show is.

Right now, "Chicago" is very hot. If you were auditioning for "Chicago" you might want to come in looking very sexy. You might wear fishnet stocking and heels with a little more makeup than you would normally wear. Again, know the show and use a little common sense. If you came to an audition for "The Sound of Music" dressed like "Chicago" it would be hard to take you seriously. I know that some of this sounds funny but I can't tell you the number of dancers that will do this. I love dancers, I love their energy, personalities and their bodies are in great shape but sometimes they just don't use their heads. They don't think about what is appropriate, they just think everyone will see how talented they are. I might be able to recognize your talent but I can guarantee you many producers won't.

DM: *I'm always looking for ways that dancers can make more money. I know in theater, especially Equity theater, there are line captains, dance captains and certain roles that a dancer might move into. How do you select these positions?*

RB:  I look for someone that is reliable. That may sound easy but very often it isn't. I need someone that is on time. Someone that never marks the combination but always does it full out. I cannot tolerate marking. I have to have someone that gets along well with the other cast members. They don't have to be best friends with everyone but just gets along well. The other thing I can't tolerate is gossip. I need someone that doesn't gossip. It can kill the cast morale and dancers are very good at it. See, you can tell I've been around a long time and I know dancers. I love dancers that absolutely do their best every time they perform. There are dancers that really try to help other dancers, not in a show-off way but with a kindness and a love that I really admire.

DM: *Most dancers I know hate to sing. What can you tell them to help through the process?*

RB:  I wish there were some magic answer but the truth is study, study, study. There were no real shortcuts with dance and there aren't any with singing. Get with a good vocal coach and study. Learn to sight-read a little bit if you can, play piano if you can. I love to learn anything in the arts so it's easy for me to say that you must study. Most dancers hate to sing because they can't do it. The physicality in singing is very different from dance. With dance your brain and your body are very busy doing the steps. Singing is much less physical and a little more intellectual and that makes dancers nervous. If you study and you have a little confidence in what you're doing, you'll find it's easier to handle the nerves. It's the same with dance, if you're in class all week working on pirouettes and you have an audition on Saturday, when you set up for that pirouette you are confident you're going to hit it because you've been practicing all week. It's the same thing with singing.

I don't like to generalize but I can give dancers a tip for a singing audition. Investigate the lyrics of the song and sing with emotion. Most dancers don't sing with emotion or they sing with the same emotion no matter what song they're singing. If it's "Mary had a little Lamb" or "Phantom of the Opera" they sing with the same emotion. Go to the lyrics, select the appropriate emotion and really show me the emotion. It's what we are really looking for. If you want to do musical theater you must sing, dance, and act, so study.

DM: *What are some mistakes that dancers make at auditions that really make you crazy?*

RB:  Oh my, let me think. When dancers come in to an audition to sing, we always put a mark on the floor where we want them to stand. This mark is usually about 15 feet away so we can see a full length shot of them. Many dancers will go right past the mark and lean on the table and put their face right in your face and sing a song. This is a mistake. It takes all the attention off of the dancer and just makes everyone uncomfortable. Don't do it.

When they read a section of the script and I say "That was good, now can you try it this way", and they do it exactly the same way again. Dancers are used to taking direction with dance, make sure you take direction with acting and singing. Very often, they are so nervous they just shake their head okay, but you know they really didn't hear a word I said. Please, take direction and make an effort to make the changes I asked for. If you continue to do it the same way over and over again, I know this is a performer that I won't be able to work with. Many directors and choreographers will love what you did and give you a correction on purpose, just to see if you listen and can make the change.

Another thing I want to say to minimize audition mistakes is, don't offer a lot of information. Many times a choreographer or producer will ask a question. Just answer the question. Many dancers will be so nervous they will continue on talking about their dog and their cousin or whatever. It works sometimes but most of the time it is a hindrance. Just answer the question. If a choreographer asks about your resumé, just give them your best credits.

Above all, don't lie! You will be caught if you lie. I've had dancers come in and tell me about a show they did and I was the choreographer. I know they didn't do that show. If they're lying about that what else on their resumé is a lie. Don't ever lie.

DM: *You were a dancer that had a great dance career. Now that you are on the other side of the fence, so to speak, what do you really want dancers to know about the people that do the hiring?*

RB: When I was a dancer, many times I would go into an audition thinking that the people on the other side of the table were the enemies. They're not! They want you to be good. They want you to be THE ONE. Auditioning is a very long process and they want their day to be over and successful too. Look at them as friends. Actors are told to love the camera, the camera is your friend. Well, you have to do the same thing. Think of those people behind the table as your best friends and we will see that come across. So, know that these people want to see you succeed, they do not want to see you fail. Get that image out of your head. I also want dancers to know that the best thing they can do for their own career is to be prepared.

Come in to the audition on time.

Don't be in a rush, relax and try to enjoy the process.

Make sure your music is in good condition. I've had people bring in music the pianist couldn't even read.

Don't come in with an attitude. Leave your problems outside, even if you've had to wait for a while.

Be prepared and enjoy. If you do those two things your career has a far greater chance of being a long and successful one.

*DM: Thanks Rob!*

I know I haven't talked about a specific place of work in this chapter and there are a lot of reasons for that. My first reason is that theater work varies greatly depending on what type of theater you are working in. Dinner Theaters are all over the country and can pay anywhere from $150/wk for the apprentice to $900/wk for a lead role in an established theater. Dinner Theater is just like it sounds, they combine dinner and a show as a way to draw in patrons. Dinner Theater will usually present well-known classic musicals. Plays such as "South Pacific"

"Damn Yankees" and "The King and I" are good examples. Acquaint yourself with the show before you audition and have a good time. These classic musicals are fun to do; you can learn a lot and make some money too.

As I said earlier Community Theater rarely pays but the value of what you'll learn makes it worth doing and you can gain experience and another credit on your resumé.

Many cities have a Civic Light Opera. This is what I refer to as Regional Theater. Regional Theater can be financially rewarding as well as a great place to work. Often Regional Theaters will alternate between putting on a local production and having a National Tour fill their theater. Either show can be beneficial for the dancer. Many National Tours will hold an audition in each city. There is no better way to perfect your auditioning skills then by going to auditions and who knows, you may end up being hired to tour the country with the show.

Equity Theater is what it is all about. Many dancers dream of dancing on Broadway and they are right because there is nothing quite like it. Broadway and other Equity houses have the best of everything. The most current musicals, the most professional lighting, sound, musicians, and costumes that money can buy. Oh yes, and they also pay the best. A dancer working at Equity minimum can make over $1,100 a week. But working Broadway is about more than money. God, did I just say that? Yes, as much as I love to be paid, dancing on Broadway is about fulfilling a dream. You have to work so hard and study so many different things to become an Equity dancer. This is one of the reasons "A Chorus Line" was so successful. So few dancers get lucky enough to dance on an Equity stage but I wish everyone could know the feeling of performing in a grand new musical. So, start studying now, it can all happen for you.

I'm sure many of you know the local theaters in your area. If not, search them out. Remember that Patsy Swayze said, "Don't go to NY or LA until you have performed every type of work in your area". You will learn so much by doing a local play. The auditions are in your local paper and there is a good chance your dance teacher knows the people running the audition. If you are a dancer already in NY or LA, you must do theater and showcases to help your career. Dance agents in both cities will confirm this. Both cities have all kinds of theater available, Dinner Theater, Regional Theater, Summer Stock, Equity Waiver (this is where the stage union, Equity, allows union actors to waive their salary to showcase their talent). Actors are used to working on stage to stay sharp, stay in front of an audience and have industry people come to see their work. Dancers must do the same! You will find theatrical auditions in "Backstage" in New York and "Backstage West" in Los Angeles. Doing theater is a must for every dancer.

# Chapter Ten

# Where's The Ballet?

Can you talk about the history of literature without mentioning Shakespeare? Can you explain how Western languages developed and not mention Latin? And yet, here I am writing about career possibilities for dancers, and I haven't discussed ballet companies. I've agonized about this section for months. When I first began researching ballet I realized I was going to have a problem. There are hundreds of ballet companies nationwide. The number of companies isn't as frightening as the diversity. There are professional or union companies, secondary and regional ballet companies. Universities have companies, civic ballets and even large dance schools form their own ballet companies. To truly do ballet justice, I would need to write a whole book on the subject. Really!

Thank God, someone has. There are so many differences in terms of scholarships, pay, performances, rehearsals and class. To discuss these differences would not be practical. Let me show you why. The focus of this book is to inform about <u>non–union</u> work that young dancers will find easier to get when they're starting out, but when it comes to ballet companies, the secondary companies are just <u>too</u> different. Some companies pay, some don't.  Most companies give you training and the opportunity to perform in lieu of money.

Some secondary companies hire professional dancers seasonally with a troupe of non–professional in the corps. The variations are staggering!

Another problem is longevity.  In Europe, many ballet companies are subsidized by their government.  In the U.S., ballet companies have to <u>apply</u> for grants and <u>hope</u> for private donations.  As our government reduces the amount of money available to the arts, many companies have been hit hard.

Now don't get depressed.  There are new companies forming all the time and ballet will always be around, but from a research point of view, the rapidity of change makes some information obsolete before it gets to print.

Last reason:  I've covered many topics I feel have been neglected by other authors, but ballet has been covered <u>extensively</u>, and information about ballet companies is all around you.  I'm going to take a gamble and say that I'll bet I can find a dance school in the U.S. that doesn't have any knowledge of what a dancer's life is like in a Japanese production.

I'd also be willing to wager that there isn't a qualified dance studio in the U.S. that doesn't have an abundance of information about nearby ballet companies and probably has contacts there.  It stands to reason that teachers know about ballet companies, most dance teachers have performed in professional and secondary companies.  But—how many dance teachers across the U.S. have danced in music videos, or on cruise lines?

But I'm not going to wimp out on ballet dancers!

I want you to know about the most in-depth book on American and European Ballet Companies that I have ever seen.  The American edition is called just that, "The Dance Directory of Ballet Companies", American

Edition". This book and its European counterpart have everything you need to know about every major and smaller ballet company in the country. An example of how it lists each company is as follows:

Name and address of ballet company
Name and background of Artistic Director
Name of ballet Mistress or Master
Teachers
Number of dancers in company
Length of dancers contract
Salary, bonuses and extra performance pay if applicable.
How many performances a year

## Audition Requirements

Height requirements for male and female,
Photographs required – (usually headshot and full body shot)
Resumé
City audition will be held in and when
Where audition will be advertised
Is there an Apprenticeship program?

Every question you could possibly have is answered in this book. The book is written by Faith Shaw Petrides and is updated each and every year. Faith has also put together another book, which will tell you the time and dates of every ballet company audition. This book is called "The Dance Directory Audition Calendar". It lists dance company auditions by date, starting at the beginning of the year just like a calendar. You can look through week by week and find out which companies are holding their auditions, what they are looking for and how much the registration fee is. Three unbelievably informative books and, as Faith will tell you, keeping this up to date is a full time job. I will tell you more about Faith Shaw Petrides in "Welcome to the New Milennium". You see,

Faith has a terrific web site on the Internet where you can get all this information and more.

I've decided to once again give you an example of what the best is offering and allow you to judge all other companies accordingly.

I contacted AGMA (The American Guild of Musical Artists). AGMA is the guild representing professional ballet companies. AGMA not only covers dancers but Apprentices, Narrators, Singers, choreographers, stage managers and stage directors. AGMA has a fifty page National Dance Basic Agreement, but don't worry. I'll just give you the highlights of the agreement.

## Bonds

Bonds are just one way AGMA protects the ballet dancer. A professional dance company must put up a bond at least one week before any rehearsal, engagement, or any travel to an engagement may take place. The security bond will be paid by the Employer to AGMA. If the ballet company is an established company the bond will be one week's salary for the members of the company. If a ballet company suddenly folded, the dancers would receive their last week's check.

## Compensation

Minimum compensation – Rehearsal/Performance weeks

| | |
|---|---|
| Apprentice | $285.00 |
| New Dancer | $570.00 |
| Corps Dancer | $727.00 |
| Solo Dancer | $786.00 |
| Principal Dancer | $852.00 |

It doesn't stop there. Professional Ballet companies have negotiated:

**Overtime pay** – an hourly rate of around $30 payable in one–half hour increments.

**Travel overtime** – an hourly rate of around $20 payable in one–half hour increments if your travel happens to take longer than expected or you're forced to travel on what would normally be your free day.

**Extraordinary Risk Pay** – a rate of $40 for each on–stage technical rehearsal, dress rehearsal and each performance that a dancer performs four feet above the stage, suspended from a wire or on stilts or ramps.

**Per Diem** – will be paid to any dancer required to be more than 30 miles from the in–city departure point. Per Diem is around $40.

## Rehearsal

A rehearsal week shall mean a Monday through Sunday week. It will consist of five rehearsal days and two free days. Rehearsal weeks do not need to be consecutive. Other rehearsals can include:

**Emergency rehearsal** – a rehearsal necessitated by the inability of a dancer to perform due to sickness or injury.

**Spill–over rehearsals** – which means an unscheduled rehearsal of the same ballet. Spill–over rehearsal shall not exceed one–half hour per day.

**Dress Rehearsal** – a rehearsal which includes the following elements:

1. All performing Artists shall appear in full costume and makeup.

2. All scenery, lighting, props and costumes are utilized.

3. Full orchestra utilized.

4. No printed program or program credits.

## Performance

The Artist may be required to take part in not more than seven performances per week on tour and not more than eight performances per week in the city of origination.

A demonstration shall count as one–half performance providing that the total elapsed time including travel does not exceed 4 hours and that each demonstration does not exceed 50 minutes. If you perform back to back demonstrations they must not exceed 50 minutes and must have a rest period of 25 minutes between. It's equivalent to one full performance.

The following topics and many others have been negotiated and agreed upon by producers and AGMA:

Travel – Bus, Air or Train Royalties
Hotels                     Costume fittings
Photographic calls         Medical benefits
Seniority                  Master classes

The Guild has left nothing to chance when it comes to protecting the ballet dancer. Whether you've just been hired to perform with ABT, dance in the corps of a regional ballet company or dance locally just for the fun of it, you should be aware of AGMA's basic dance agreement to protect dancers.

**AGMA**
1727 Broadway, Second Floor
New York City, NY 10019-5284
(212) 265-3687

## Chapter Eleven

# Dance Rags

I wanted to include a chapter where you could get behind the scene information on dance magazines and dance newspapers. The reason is, I want you to know in what type of information each magazine specializes. This way, no matter what part of the country you live in, you can subscribe to the dance magazine that suits your interests.

For the longest time there was just "Dance Magazine," an informative magazine for dancers. In the past "Dance Magazine" has been known for its information for the ballet dancer and the ballet company. However, it is now starting to branch out and cover work in other areas of dance. There's an exceptional new section of the magazine called "Young Dancer" and I found it to be honest and right on target. It calls for young dancers to be realistic when they evaluate their own talent. It has articles that encourage preparation, versatility, and training – the same attributes every choreographer wants to see from a dancer when they audition. Today there are many magazines informing the dancer. "Dance Teacher Now" specializes in informing the teacher on new techniques, and how to run their studios better. "Backstage" and "Backstage West", are well known trade papers in the New York and Los Angeles areas. They are very informative on the job market and any dancer moving to New York should pick one up before they unpack. The last few examples are all well done but also well known. I want to inform you of great information you may not be aware of. I will cover a magazine, a newspaper and a couple of Internet web sites where you can search out the information you are looking for.

## DANCE AND FITNESS WEST

I want to start by introducing you to Grover Dale. Yes, Grover is the President of the L.A. Dance Foundation and yes, he is the senior editor of Dance and Fitness West Magazine. It's also very easy for me to say that Grover is actively involved in developing new musical projects for the stage and screen. If I were to stop there I wouldn't be honoring an amazing dance career. You see, I know from experience that if you tell dancers that a guy is the senior editor of Dance and Fitness West Magazine, they'll think he did that all his life. When I tell young hopefuls that I wrote a book for dancers looking to pursue a career in dance, they say, "Great, did you ever dance?"

Well, yes, I did have a nice dance career but not nearly as prolific as Grover Dale's . He has performed, directed, written and choreographed for the stage, film and television. He is the recipient of the Tony Award, the Drama Desk Award, the Dramalogue Award, an Emmy and multiple Clio Awards. He has been involved with sixteen Broadway musicals, eight motion pictures and over eighty-five television productions. Some of his performing highlights include the original cast of "West Side Story" and a featured dance role and understudy to Anthony Perkins in "Greenwillow".

As a choreographer, he was nominated for a Tony Award and won the Drama Desk Award for Choreography, in the production of "Billy". He co-choreographed "Seesaw" with Michael Bennett and this time took home the Tony Award. As a co-director with Jerome Robbins, Grover won the Tony Award for Directorial Achievement for a production every dancer wanted to be in, "Jerome Robbins Broadway". As you can see, he hasn't been senior editor of Dance and Fitness West all of his life. So, I asked him how this groundbreaking magazine came to be.

His first idea was to start a newsletter, in order to inform dancers and other choreographers about what was going on in town. It was called the LA Dance Foundation and it was never Grover's intention to start a magazine. What started out in 1992 as a newsletter for 125 people has turned into Dance and Fitness West with 30,000 people benefiting from its "bare fisted approach to the real, the relevant, and the useful" (part of their marketing slogan).

DM: *Why did you take on a tough assignment like putting out this magazine?*

GD: You know it's funny, but my background as a dancer really helped me in business and I think it's the same for all dancers. We don't think of ourselves as business people but we are running our own businesses when we start out on our dance careers. We're used to getting up in the morning and taking care of our business. If we don't get out there and do it, it will not get done. I feel the same way about choreography. It was a perfect background for putting together a magazine. I was used to being creative and the structure of choreography helped me put things together. With choreography, you visualize something and then you go about making it happen. There were no books on how to put together a magazine but when you think about it, there aren't any books on performing either. We all have to find our own way.

*DM: So, you just kind of improvised as you went along?*

GD: Again, as performers we are used to improvising and thinking on our feet. Especially when problems come up. I remember one night I was in the production of "Greenwillow" and I was playing the devil. I would go on stage, pull a cookie out of a jar and tempt a little kid with it. One night I went on stage, reached into the jar and there wasn't any cookie. I had to make it work right on the spot and come up with something. This is really good training for business. You just handle the problems as they come up.

*DM: If you didn't want to do a magazine, how did the whole thing happen?*

GD: At first, The Society of Stage Directors and Choreographers were helping to fund the newsletter. We had no intention of it growing, we just wanted to inform the dance community in Hollywood. At a particular point the SSDC couldn't help fund it any longer and we thought that might be the end of the newsletter. What happened was a few of the board members on SSDC decided to take out personal ads in the newsletter, for a fee. We then decided if we can sell a few more ads, the newsletter might pay for itself. The ads continued to grow and brought in income. What started out as a liability and almost an end to the newsletter turned into an asset and the growth we've seen to this point.

*DM: I guess that is improvisation. What was your original intention for content in this expanding magazine?*

GD: Many of us could see that a lot of the dance community had no idea about the auditioning process. You could just see it. They didn't know how producers worked and how they fit into the big picture. They didn't know how to market or showcase themselves, and they didn't know how to train or draw attention to themselves at auditions. We had this information and there became a need to share it and get it to the dancer.

*DM: And this policy remains today?*

GD: There is only one policy when it comes to writing articles for Dance and Fitness West. There are only educational pieces, and no cosmetic pieces. If it's not educational you won't see it in the magazine.

*DM: If I was to ask you to name one thing that makes your magazine different than the others, what would you say that is?*

GD: We're dancers! We're authentic! Words come out differently if you're a businessperson or a professional writer. We may not be as articulate as a professional writer is, but they can't write like a dancer either. The articles that we write, who we are and the way we write them is a major reason for our success. Dancers can relate to the magazine because it's like talking to another dancer.

*DM: Thank you Grover.*

If you're interested in an educational dance magazine and a lot more, consider a subscription to Dance and Fitness West. There is always a section on dance classes in Los Angeles and Tony Selznick's column "The Buzz" gives the dancer an insight on working choreographers, showcases and award shows. Grover Dale and assistant editor Mary Miller write an exceptional column and Larry Billman's articles on the history of dance are second to none.

If you are interested in subscribing to LA Dance and Fitness West, write to:

**Dance and Fitness West**
627 N. Palm Dr.
Beverly Hills, Ca 90210

## THE DIRT ALERT

Once again before discussing the newspaper, I want to give you the background on another amazing dancer/choreographer that felt the need to fill a void, to help other dancers, and start a new business all at the same time.

To those of you reading and wondering what it takes to be successful in dance, look deep into the stories about these special dancer/choreographers. They all started their careers the same way. They studied dance at a local studio and they had dreams of dancing on-stage, in film, and on television. They had dreams of dancing **anywhere,** for any amount of money as long as they could pay the bills and continue to dance. Minnie Madden started just that way, but I want to show you where her persistence and training eventually took her.

She started in a small local studio, studied hard and eventually went to New York, like thousands of dancers before her. She won a scholarship with the Alvin Ailey Dance Company and that began an impressive fifteen-year professional dance career. She worked for Michael Peters on the NBC Emmy Awards. She danced on the AGVA Awards with choreographer Jerry Jackson and performed in the Radio City Music Hall Easter Show, choreographed by Peter Genero. A versatile and disciplined dancer, Minnie began to choreograph. She choreographed "Applause", starring Phyllis McGuire, "Madam Goes to Harlem," starring Wayland Flowers, and became the resident choreographer at the Sahara Hotel, in Las Vegas. At the Sahara, she choreographed the "Sahara Girls". The "Sahara Girls" were a line of dancers who were to become the opening act for many celebrities including Johnny Carson, Don Rickles, Frank Sinatra, Buddy Hackett, Jerry Lewis, George Carlin and many others. The "Sahara Girls" even had the opportunity to perform on the "Tonight Show".

As a director/choreographer, Minnie started to work ice-skating shows and to this day has choreographed over twenty major ice show productions. These productions include big name skaters like Tai Babilonia, Randy Gardner, Nicole Bobek, Oksana Baiul, Brian Boitano, and Viktor Petrenko. Minnie recently served as President of Productions for the Ice Capades. Not bad for a dancer that doesn't even ice skate. I'm telling you this for two reasons. First to give you some background and insight into Minnie Madden's career and second, to show you that if you're well trained, versatile and willing to go for it, your dance career can take you anywhere.

Now that I've brought you up-to-date, let's retrace our steps a little and I'll tell you about the Dirt Alert. The Dirt Alert is an "entertainment job employment newspaper". It is printed in Las Vegas and is distributed nationally. It was started by Minnie in the spring of 1989.

DM: *Minnie, how and why did you decide to start the "Dirt Alert"?*

MM: I came to Las Vegas from New York and like any dancer I went in search of "Backstage", you know, the newspaper in New York for dancers and other people in the industry that helps them find work.

DM: *And what did you find?*

MM: Nothing! That's the point, they didn't have anything like that. I kept hearing, "Las Vegas, the entertainment capitol of the world", and they don't even have an industry newspaper. All auditions at that point were either at the studios or word of mouth. So, I started talking about an idea to start our own newsletter and everyone thought that was a great idea. One morning, I was having coffee with a friend, Mark Tan, and I told him my idea. Mark worked on the Hollywood Reporter and Variety in Los Angeles. He thought it was a great idea and was willing to work with me as an editor. That was on a Tuesday and by Saturday, we were distributing the first issue. I borrowed $2100.00 for distribution and we sent out this crooked typewritten newsletter. Oh, by the way, I've paid the $2,100 back.

DM: *How did you get it out?*

MM: My friends and I took it to agencies, dance studios and to the line captains of all the production shows in Las Vegas. I had a business license and an accountant, but no business plan or anything, just an idea.

DM: *How much was the original newsletter?*

MM: The first two issues were free. We knew we just had to get it out and let dancers see what a great thing this could be for them and the city. I think we charged $1.50 for the third issue.

DM: *Did you make money?*

MM: No! The paper didn't make any profit for the first eight years. In fact, I had to put money in quite a few times. But, we had over a hundred subscribers and we had no overhead. We were working out of the house with a "trial and error" method and we made just enough to keep it going.

DM: *If you didn't make any money, why did you keep on writing?*

MM: People were getting work! It was so exciting to get letters from dancers who were working and knowing they got the information from the paper. I even got letters from mothers saying, "My daughter has always wanted to work in a dance review and thank you so much for your work with the newsletter." It was incredible!

DM: *When did the newsletter change to the newspaper we see today?*

MM: I had a great printer early on. He was a very honest and sincere man that told me it would be cheaper if I were to print the newsletter like a newspaper. Especially now that our subscriber base was growing and I had to mail out a lot of newsletters. So I went to the local newspaper and they agreed to print our little paper. I also went to the post office and got a permit for bulk mail and off we went.

DM: *Grover Dale was just talking about how his dance and choreography background really helps in problem solving and business solutions. Would you agree with that?*

MM: Absolutely! In fact, I would even go further. I think employers should know the value of hiring dancers and ex-dancers. They're disciplined, they're hardworking, they're used to taking direction and making changes on the spot, and they know the show must go on. Dancers know how to meet a deadline. We are used to pulling it together at the last minute and making it happen. I think that type of background is needed in the corporate world.

DM: *Now, I know you're not the only owner of the Dirt Alert today. What was the reason for the changes?*

MM: I started the paper at a slow time in my career and as everyone knows as soon as you do that your career starts to take off again. I got to the point where I couldn't sell it, because I loved it and I couldn't keep it because I couldn't run it. So, I decided to sell half to two friends of mine Billy Chapel and Peter Gordon. They are both ex-skaters and they expressed interest in the paper.

DM: *It's now profitable?*

MM: Yes, it's now profitable and for the first time I would say there is an equal balance of subscribers and advertising income. Dance is a very small market so you know someone like Toyota is not going to take out ad space but we are getting our share of advertising and it's enough to keep up the paper.

DM: *With Grover Dale and Dance and Fitness West, their magazine is really directed toward education. The Dirt Alert is directed towards jobs and not article content, is that right?*

MM: Yes, right now it is an entertainment job employment paper but it is continuing to grow. I want to have educational articles. We are hiring editors for more articles and I want to expand to musicians and stagehands. I want to have articles on acting and local health clubs. The health clubs are important to dancers as to the types of classes they offer. Health clubs are an important resource for the dancer on exercise and nutrition.

DM: *Where do you get your audition information from?*

MM: As you can imagine most of our audition information is for shows in Los Angeles and Las Vegas, but we also get auditions for a large number of foreign productions. We have now been around a while and our reputation is so good, producers from major touring shows like "Grease" and "Will Rogers Follies" are now advertising their information in the Dirt Alert. In fact, I went to Royal Caribbean Cruise Lines as a choreographer hoping to choreograph a few of their shows. When they saw that I was from Las Vegas they asked me if I knew anything about the Dirt Alert. I said, "Oh a little bit, I own it". They went on and on about the paper for over an hour. They had their audition information in the Dirt Alert and were ecstatic about the turnout. They were also very impressed that the dancers were so well prepared for the audition. They came in wearing the right thing, they had both heels and flat shoes and Royal Caribbean could hire quite a few of them. This is the number one reason for the paper. To get the correct message from the employer to the dancers, so the dancers come prepared and can get jobs. I want the paper to help **give people jobs.**

DM: *Did Royal Caribbean hire you?*

MM: I don't know! We talked so much about the Dirt Alert, I don't know if they're going to hire me. No, the interview went well but I haven't heard back yet. Oh yeah, back to jobs, we are starting to get a lot of European activity now in the paper. There are quite a few productions going to Europe and they're placing their information with us.

DM: *I think the paper is great and I want dancers to subscribe to it. How do they do that?*

MM: We are on the internet at www.dirtalert1.aol.com, so they can do it that way or they can call:

(702) 891-9222

Or they can write to:

**Dirt Alert**
2375 E. Tropicana Ave. Suite 6
Las Vegas, NV. 89119

Subscription rates (bi-weekly) Six Months – $26, One Year – $52.

## Chapter Twelve

# Welcome To The New Millennium

*"People who don't know how to use information are not going to do well in the twenty-first century."*
Joe Turow, Professor of Communications
University of Pennsylvania

I'm always trying to keep you informed on new jobs, so, I want to show you another way to search for work – with your computer!  Dance is well represented on the Internet and this may be the future of dance.  You can find a wide variety of dance web sites.  There are specific sites specializing in tap dance where dancers can talk to each other and tell other dancers about the latest show, class or tap shoes.  Just search for "The Tap Dance Homepage".  If you are interested in the competition circuit, there are now close to forty different competitions making their way across the country each weekend and you can find their schedules on another terrific site, www.danceronline.com.  There are personal web pages, complete dancewear sites, and every style of dance is represented from ballroom to modern.  But for our purposes, I want to stick to the sites that can help you find employment and a career.

## DANCE PROFESSIONALS ASSOCIATES, LTD.

### www.dancepro.com

There is a terrific web site on the Internet called Dance Professionals Associates, LTD.. For the dancer familiar with the web, its address is www.dancepro.com. This web site is run by Faith Patrides, pronounced (Patreedees). Faith was born in New York City and studied with Vera Nemtchinova at the School of American Ballet while performing in children's roles for the New York City Ballet. She continued her studies at the ABT School with Patricia Wilde, Leon Danielian, Michael Maule, Vladimir Dokoudovsky, Maggie Black, Don Farnsworth and many others. Upon retirement she returned to university and studied Arts Management. Today she has joined the staff of the New York City Ballet in the Development Department.

In 1992 Ms. Petrides began to research information that would help young dancers looking to join ballet companies. The result was the publication of "The Dance Directory of Ballet Companies", American and European editions. These Directories are updated annually and include a calendar of audition dates for companies and schools. You will not find a more complete book on ballet companies. You can find out when they hold their auditions, find out the size of the company, who is the ballet Mistress or Master? What they cost, what they require and what they pay, are all addressed on this incredible web site.

It didn't take long before Faith wanted this information to reach an even wider audience. She founded the Dance Professionals Associates, Ltd. This is an association to help all dancers with discount benefits and resources. Let me tell you just a few of the many things DPA offers. They offer an entire array of insurance plans ranging from Life Insurance, Health Insurance (both domestic and international), Dental, and an Expense Reimbursement Plan if disabled. It's about time dancers grouped together to save money on some of the insurance necessities. But it doesn't stop there, Business Overhead Insurance is available for dance companies and dance schools and this is just a portion of the membership benefits. Membership for individuals is $39.00 a year, $19.00 a year if you are under 20 years old and it includes;

- Information on audition dates
- On-line service and information via the Internet
- Listing in the DPA Internet Directory
- Personal page on the Internet (at additional cost)
- Travel Packages
- Graphic Design services
- Income Tax service
- And coming soon… a Newsletter just for Dance Professionals.

Before I get ahead of myself, let me tell you a little bit about DPA Sponsored Tours and Travel Packages. DPA is planning a tour including the 18$^{th}$ International Ballet Competition in Varna, Bulgaria. The entire tour is planned from top to bottom with transportation, hotels, most meals and motorcoach tours with English speaking guides. There will be master classes majoring in the classical repertoire for participation in International ballet Competitions.

Classical Ballet
Bournonville System
Graham-based modern technique
Jazz dance

Also included in this particular tour is a trip to Vienna, Austria where you'll enjoy a tour around the city before heading back to the states. This is just one of the major DPA tours. Another tour is a 1998 tour of Moscow, St. Petersburg and Helsinki where you'll tour the Bolshoi Theater, watch a Gala performance of the Maya Competition and visit the dance museum in St. Petersburg. These tours are once in a lifetime experiences for the dancer hoping to become a professional.

DPA is an exciting organization with terrific management. Look for the upcoming newsletter. It will be interesting to see how this web site grows in the future. I will keep you posted, but in the meantime take a few minutes and explore www.dancepro.com.

## DanceArt

**www.danceart.com**

This is a very informative web site sharing in-depth knowledge of the New York City area. David M. Wilson has put together a site that is both fun and informative. I asked David how this all came about.

DM: *David, why did you start this web site and company and where would you like to see it go?*

DW: Wow, there must be as many answers to that as there are to my starting dance at the age of 27. I'll try to summarize it for you. This site and company actually started as an attempt to build a fundraising product for a ballet studio. It was going to be a dance clipart product that the studio and the dancers could sell. I won't get into it but it didn't work out the way I had planned. Well, I had drawn too many pieces of clipart to just throw them away so I put them on a web site. So many people loved the clipart that I retained an artist and then another and the site grew.

DM: *How did you know about clipart and how to put them on the Net?*

DW: My background is in the commercial software industry. I was a software development manager for the Hallmark Card Studio Program published by Micrografx Inc. My software design role had me learning how to draw on the computer to prototype screen artwork. I was in dance classes regularly by then and I was amazed at how little dance clipart was available. The web site initially grew from a way to share free dance clipart and expanded into other features because I thought it would be fun.

DM: *Well, you can tell that because the site certainly is fun but a way to pass out free clipart wasn't the only motivation factor, was it?*

DW: No, I always enjoy eliminating barriers that prevent computer-shy people from getting comfortable with the technology. The web site and dance topic was obviously enough to interest girls in computers and software so they could participate in something they love. This merging of a female friendly site, dance and technology can keep me talking for days.

DM: *Although the site is wonderful, you are making improvements constantly?*

DW: Yes, I started the site in September of 1996. I was determined to offer a safe chat environment and coded my own in July 1997. We have already outgrown it. The dance job listings reside in this original chat section. By upgrading the chat section and moving it, I will be able to improve the job section. In the last few months, feature design on the site has begun to be directed by a larger growth plan. I want to provide technical solutions for other dance sites, build traffic and grow the sites, so, I have created dance guest books, a dance web ring (to connect dance sites) and I've created the Dance Chat Network. Each component can be used by other web sites and integrates into our dance schools database. The next major push is to fully address dance products and advertisers that need exposure on the site – exactly the sort of exposure you are looking for with this book.

Thank you David for the hard work and the terrific dance web site. We look forward to seeing its growth in the future. David gave us a nice inside look on how danceart.com got started and where it is headed but let me tell you a little bit more about what is currently available on the site.

Dancers can read current articles on dance, get lists of dance classes in New York and stay up on new dance shows and their reviews. There is an advice column, interviews with celebrities, and even a message and chat room. (If you're new to the computer, a chat room is an area where people can talk about a common topic, live, on the Internet.) This web site also offers a free newsletter! All you have to do is enter your information and the newsletter will keep you up to date on New York City happenings.

For our purposes, the web site has a job page. If you are a producer, you can post your audition notices. If you are a dancer looking for work, not only can you browse through the audition and employment ads, but you can also input your qualifications and job seeking desires. I have to say, right now the page on employment is mainly geared toward studios needing teachers but if we get the word out, I think more employers will put their audition information on the site. Either way, a dancer can utilize the job information on danceart.com because many dancers supplement their income by teaching.

Let me give an example of articles you'll find on danceart.com. "Beyond the Barre" written by Sondra Forsythe, encourages dancers coming to New York City to not just take class but see the city. You should take in the cultural resources NYC has to offer. The museums, the Zoo and Broadway are all fun to see and the site is equipped with a "city search" icon, which is constantly updated with information.

Sondra also informs dancers of exciting summer programs. These programs are intensive seminars that dancers may not be aware of. In this particular article she highlights, "Ballet Academy East. The article on Ballet Academy East is complete with faculty, classes and tuition.

DanceArt is constantly working on a Ballet and Dance web ring. This is where other new and exciting web sites can join the web ring. With this web ring, if what you're looking for isn't available at one site, with one click of your mouse you can search the web ring and probably find what you need.

New York Dance Scene is one of my favorite pages on danceart.com. There is so much information about New York City. There are tips on dance classes, audition information, private teachers, where to stay, getting around town and fixing your resumé. I'm just highlighting what's on this website but I think that's plenty. If you want more, I encourage you to go and explore danceart.com for yourself. It's great!

## SOUTHERN CALIFORNIA DANCE AND DIRECTORY

**www.usc.edu/dept/dance/**

Southern California Dance and Directory is a directory of professional dance companies and service organizations. Louise Reichlin, Mary Kat Kennedy and Deep "Kim" Singh developed this site. Not being able to cover everything, they have some in-depth information on local dance companies. Some examples are University of Southern California, Los Angeles Choreographers and Dancers and Zapped Taps/Alfred Desio. The site has an amazing listing of links to other dance sites. There is information on a ton of other Dance Companies. There are sites about choreographers, schools, music and ballroom dance. There are links to Dance Agents representing both choreographers and dancers. The Dance Resource Center and the Dance Alliance are listed and there is even a site to help dancers make the transition out of dance and into another career when the time comes.

There is a job section, but once again it is centered on teaching positions. I think the time has come for a website with just audition information. Hmmm, that may be my next project. Anyway, visit Southern California Dance and Directory. With a little work you can find absolutely anything you need in regards to dance.

# THE ROCKETTES

**www.radiocity.com**

Oh, how I wanted to do a whole chapter dedicated to becoming a Rockette. In the past, thousands of dancers have danced at Radio City Music Hall and thousands more have dreamed of dancing there. I made at least twenty calls over a three-month period to the home office in New York. I talked to the Director of Operations, who then passed me down to Ruth Sarfaty in Public Relations. They were very pleasant and cooperative but nothing would happen. I would call back for information and they told me they would send it out immediately, but nothing came. I would send a fax with the information I needed outlined. Nothing! This went on for over three months. I know this is a very busy organization but I would think that getting the word out to dancers interested in becoming Rockettes would be a priority. Well, the book was almost complete and I just couldn't wait any longer. I've never been good at accepting defeat so I went to the Internet to try to find information on my own. Radio City Productions has a well-organized informative site right on the web. Someone could have told me! But that's okay, I found it and I'm going to tell you about it and where you can find this terrific site. Very simply, www.radiocity.com will give you a history on the Rockettes, worldwide scheduling, how to get tickets and where all the new productions will be in the future.

## Background

The Rockettes have been around since 1925 where they started out as the Missouri Rockets. A New York producer named Roxy Rothafe bought the production for his Roxy Theater and changed the name to the Roxyettes. When the Music Hall was built they became the Rockettes. Today, there are over 175 women dancing as Rockettes and the projection is that there will be more soon.

The web site has an excellent virtual tour of the Music Hall Theater. You can get a look at the stage and learn about the history of the stage, theater and the architect that put it all together.

You can learn about Radio City Productions. Remember our chapter on Production Companies, well, Radio City Productions is a major production company producing not just the Rockettes but sports spectaculars, movie debuts and television specials. They promote many other shows including, Barney, Lord of the Dance, Riverdance, Disney on Ice and many others. But far and away their most successful show is The Radio City Christmas Spectacular. The Radio City Christmas Spectacular is the number one show in America and continues to break box office records. It has broken its own box office record for the last 17 years in a row. In an eight week holiday run The Radio City Christmas Spectacular brings in more people than Broadway does for an entire year. This record setting show doesn't look like it will end anytime soon. In fact, this year Christmas Productions are being planned for Detroit, Chicago, Myrtle Beach, Branson and Los Angeles. Plus, a troupe of Rockettes also tour the country performing at sporting events, concerts and on Film and Television. What this means for the dancer is more and more young women will get to fulfill their dream of becoming a Rockette.

## How to become a Rockette

This section on their web site is probably in need of the most work. There is very little information available but I will tell you what I've learned. You must be 18 years of age and between 5'5½" and 5'9" tall. You must be proficient in jazz and tap.

I have spoken with many current Rockettes and they've told me, "When they say proficient, they really mean it." I also know many quality dancers that have auditioned for the Rockettes numerous times and have not been successful. This is a very selective organization and you should be aware of that. But don't get discouraged, as I said earlier with the opening of new productions, Radio City Productions will need to hire more Rockettes.

Radio City Productions is actively seeking a multi-cultural group of women. This is a very nice way of saying that they are looking for Black, Hispanic, Asian and other minorities to audition. This wasn't always the case. For many years, the Rockettes were primarily Caucasian and like a Vegas Showgirl line, many minorities weren't hired. Consequently, minority dancers stopped showing up at their auditions because they figured they didn't have a chance. Well, that has all changed I'm happy to report and both Vegas and Radio City are looking for all types to come to their auditions.

One thing hasn't changed though, and that is weight. Although very few people will come out and say it because they want to be politically correct, weight is still a major issue for dancers today. I know a few excellent dancers that have been turned down by Radio City because of their weight. These dancers are not overweight by the normal world's standard but may be overweight in the dance world. This is not a pleasant topic and people are very opinionated about it, but the truth is, I have talked with many producers about dancers' weight problems and although some of them will never admit it, they have told me privately that a dancer's weight is a major concern. No matter how they feel personally, they can not hire dancers that are overweight. If you are a dancer that struggles with a weight problem, try to sensibly work on it now. No one wants to see an anorexic dancer or a dancer become bulimic, so teachers refuse to tell students to work on their weight. I've had dancers perform for me and then ask me what they should work on to become a professional dancer. Knowing what I'm told from the people that do the hiring, I have to tell them that the best thing they can do for their career is to work on their weight. It's not what a lot of people want to hear but at this date and time, unfortunately, it's the truth.

The Radio City site has a list of scheduled events and how you can get tickets. If you've never seen the Rockettes perform, you should. It is always beneficial to see a show you may be auditioning for.

Here is a Hotline number for tickets and other information: (212) 307-1000

# BACKSTAGE

## www.backstage.com

I spoke briefly about the Backstage trade paper in the Dance Rags chapter. This trade paper is one of the best and most visible employment papers in the industry. Hundreds of dancers, actors and stagehands use the paper on a weekly basis. The good news is they are also on the Internet. The Backstage web site includes the periodicals, "Backstage," "Backstage West" and "Dramalogue". Pages on this web site include jobs for the Equity Stage, non-union stage work, Film and Television work and work for the stagehand and technical staff.

The non-member only has limited access to the site. For full access you need to subscribe and become a member. You will receive you access code and this will entitle you to read their current issue of Backstage West on site at 3PM EST every Wednesday. You can also read Backstage (geared more toward NYC work) at 3PM EST every Thursday. Another nice perk to being a member is you can search their archives for articles on a particular topic you might be interested in. You can become a member for a fee of $9.95 per month. This must be put on a credit card and will be automatically deducted each month. There are pre-payment plans and you can send a check for a six-month subscription for $69.95. You can also pre-pay for a year subscription for $138.90. For questions and more information you can email them at info@backstage.com.

This is a phenomenal site and very beneficial for dancers all over the country and abroad. Think about it! If I'm dancing in a production in Guam, I can now get Backstage and Backstage West online the day it comes out.

I no longer feel as isolated out in the Pacific as I once did. I now still feel connected to the industry. As my contract is nearing completion, I can start to submit for other work and line up auditions when I return. I recently spoke with a group of Rockettes dancing at the Flamingo Hilton in Las Vegas. They were transferred from Radio City Music Hall in New York and were a little homesick for the city. They told me online Backstage keeps them connected to what's going on in New York and that's a good feeling.

These web sites cover Trade Papers, The Rockettes, Ballet, New York City and Los Angeles and yet this is just the beginning of what is on the Internet. By the New Millennium the number of dance related sites will double at least. Introducing you to these five sites was just to pique your interest and get you out there searching for yourself. There will come a time in the very near future when almost all dance audition information will be on the Internet and you'll be able to submit your dance tape over the Internet to try and secure a dance position for yourself. Actors are already on websites where Casting Directors can look at their pictures, resumés and demo-reels on the Internet and dancers won't be far behind. Even if you don't have a computer, you'll be able to use your television to access the Internet and find this information and more. Start now, it's amazing and fun to discover the amount of information at your fingertips.

# Chapter Thirteen

# Why The Unions?

I have discussed non–union work throughout this book for two reasons. One: Most young dancers will find non–union work easier to get while they're gaining experience and establishing a resumé. Two: Non–union work has the potential for more of the pitfalls discussed in the book, since guidelines and minimums haven't been established and recourse against a producer is difficult.

So what are the benefits to performing union work and why should a dancer strive to be in the union?

## Respectability

If you're a union dancer, everyone knows you've danced on commercials, TV specials, film or in Equity stage productions. A producer or director will immediately see your union affiliations at the top of your resumé and know you have experience at the union level. You'll also enjoy the benefit of being able to audition first for other union work.

**Example:** A Broadway production will audition all <u>Equity</u> dancers <u>first</u>. Only if the producer can't find what he's looking for from the union pool of dancers will he look at non–union dancers. (Well, that's not entirely true, there will always be a non-union call but the truth is, if the producers have found what they are looking for at the union call, the non-union call is just a formality.)

## Recourse

As discussed briefly in "Where's the Ballet?", a union will require a producer to put up a bond. A bond is a sum of money held by the union to insure the dancer of some payment. The bond is usually equivalent to one week's salary of the cast. If a producer closes the production and doesn't pay the dancers, the bond will be forfeited by the producer and dispensed to the dancers. In the days before the unions, the dancers would not only be out the last week's check, but if they were on the road, they'd have to find a way to get home.

Another, more serious type of recourse is litigation. A non–union dancer that has not received payment will find it difficult and expensive to try to sue a producer. The Guild has lawyers on staff that will attempt to litigate for union members. I said attempt because even union lawyers have a difficult time.

## Horror Story!

Let's say, I'm going to produce a play in San Diego. I form "Green Eyes Production Co.", and produce the show. A month into the run, ticket sales are not going well. I am unable to pay back investors. I owe dancers, actors, crews, the theater, advertisers, everybody! I close the show. Green Eyes Productions declares bankruptcy, dissolves, and is difficult to sue. Three months later, I open Blue Eyes Productions and try again.

That's show biz!

These production companies are earmarked in the membership magazine. When you're hired by a production company, and it's a union job, call the union and ask if the production company is in good standing with the union.

## Negotiated Minimums

The Guilds have negotiated minimums for every job covered under their jurisdiction. If you're working in a dinner theater with 300 seats, or a Broadway show with 1700 seats, there are minimum salaries that cannot be violated. You'll hear minimums referred to as "scale". The unions will not let scale payment to the performer be violated, which is how the phrase "scale plus ten" came about. A producer will have to pay scale *plus* the extra ten percent for agent fees. The minimum salaries generally increase a small amount annually.

## Medical Benefits

Equity, AFTRA and SAG have medical and dental plans for qualifying members. I have qualified for and utilized SAG and AFTRA plans. Believe me, they have quality plans that sure help when you have an emergency. The problem is, like all insurance policies, they've gotten more and more expensive. Hospital fees, doctor fees and the onslaught of the Aids epidemic have taken a toll on union insurance policies. Not too long ago, an AFTRA member had to earn $2,000 in a year to qualify for medical and dental benefits for the member and their family. Today, that number is $7,500, and the dental plan for spouses and children has been dropped completely. Equity (the stage union), also hard hit, has increased the number of weeks you'll need to work before you're eligible for benefits. SAG has maintained their medical and dental policies, but the eligibility minimums continue to rise. Minimums are $7,500 now with rumors of $10,000 soon.

## Pensions

The unions have created pension funds for members. Can you imagine, a <u>dancer</u> with a retirement fund! The producers have agreed to pay a percentage of monies paid in salary into the members' pension fund. If a member earns a certain amount of money in a year, the union considers that <u>one</u> qualifying year. Right now, a member needs <u>ten</u> qualifying years to become vested and receive a minimum pension after age 55, (early retirement). Of course, if you have larger salaries during qualifying years, or more than ten qualifying years, your pension will increase accordingly.

## Residuals

Without a doubt, one of my favorite topics. Once you receive your first residual payment, it'll be your favorite, too. You never really know when a residual is coming, so its always a little surprise from heaven.

Residuals are not a gift and did not come about without a fight. I think you should know a little bit about the history of residuals. In 1971, the Guild felt it wasn't fair for producers to reuse programming again and again without compensating the Guild member. After a difficult negotiation process, residuals began in 1974. In 1979, the cable field was emerging, and producers found residual payments to once again be a priority with the Guild. Unable to reach what the Guild felt was fair, they voted to strike. The SAG strike lasted four months from July 21 to October 23.

The sacrifices other Guild members made in the past allow us to enjoy today's residuals.

Here's a <u>very</u> simplistic explanation of how residuals happen and how the Guild monitors them.

For a network television show rerun on network television, you will receive a percentage of your original salary. Each time the show is played the percentage will decrease. I just received a residual payment of $64.00 for a television program I worked on over eight years ago. Commercial residuals are similar with one exception. A national commercial will pay a certain amount for the original shoot, and like a television show, your residual percentage will decrease as your commercial is rerun. Unlike television shows, after a 13 week period, if your commercial is picked up (or bought again), the residual percentage will again start at the top. The other difference between a television show and a commercial, is your commercial will likely run on all three networks, giving you a greater potential for many more residuals. So, how does the Guild keep track of every member's residual payment? When a sponsor purchases air time to show their commercial, they must also pay the actors who performed in that spot. The Guild receives lists of all commercial air time purchased on any given day.

For film, it's a little more difficult. If you perform in a made for TV movie, the residual payment is similar to a television show. If you perform in a film first shown at the movie theater and later shown on TV, the network producers purchase the film for a certain amount of money. The actors collectively receive 2% of this purchase price. That 2% is then paid to the actors according to how much they made on the original shoot. Example: an actor who made $10,000 on the original shoot will get a higher percentage of the TV residual than an actor who made $7,500.

Again, this is an over–simplified explanation of how the union monitors residuals, but it should give some insight into the process.


## Other Benefits

There are many other benefits to being a member of the unions and I'll briefly mention some of them.

Credit Union – You can join the AFTRA–SAG or Equity credit union and establish checking accounts, savings accounts, credit cards, ATM cards, or apply for low–interest home, car or personal loans.

Hotlines – The Guilds have established hotlines that you can call to receive information on auditions, meetings or current Guild proceedings.

Agents – There is an indirect but important benefit to dancers becoming union members in terms of getting an agent. Many dancers cross over into acting and having union affiliation makes it a little easier to get seen by agents. Many SAG–franchised agents will not see anyone that doesn't possess a SAG card.

Classes and Showcases – You can sign up for a special class or seminar given by the Guild for its members. There are also showcase nights, where you can prepare a scene for working casting directors.

Every dancer should strive for union affiliation. Union affiliation gives you credibility, many benefits and the opportunity to audition for the best work available to dancers.

## Joining a Union

The following information explains how you can join the unions, what membership fees are, and how current dues are calculated.

### Screen Actors Guild (SAG)

5757 Wilshire Blvd.
Los Angeles, CA  90036-3635
Tel: (213)954-1600
Membership Fee: $1,060.00

Union Dues: – depend on previous year earnings. Minimum is $85 a year for earning 0 – 5,000 dollars

How to Join: – You must perform union work prior to joining.
Call for appointment. L.A. (213) 456–4000  N.Y. (212) 944–1030

### American Federation of Television and Radio Artists (AFTRA)

5757 Wilshire Blvd., 9th Floor
Los Angeles, California, 90036-3689
Tel: (213)634-8100

Membership Fee: $1,000.00

Union Dues: $42.50 every six months.

How to Join:  AFTRA is an open union.  You do not need to perform union work prior to being able to join. You'll need to go to an AFTRA office, fill out an application, and pay initial fees and first 6 month dues for a total of $1042.50

**Actor's Equity Association**
**(AEA)**
1560 Broadway
New York, NY 10036-1525
Tel: (212)869-8530

Membership Fee: $800.00

Union Dues: $39.00 every six months. If you joined SAG or AFTRA first (your parent union) and you are current with them, Equity gives you a five dollar break on dues, or $34.00 every 6 months.

How to Join: Equity has two different ways to join.

1) If you're hired to perform an Equity production, bring your contract to Equity and apply. A major benefit to joining this way is, Equity will take part of your salary weekly and you won't have to pay all the fees up–front.

2) If your Parent union is SAG and you've made a certain amount of money in a certain year, you are eligible to join Equity if you choose. This specific monetary amount increases each year; $1348 in 1992, $1428 in 1993, etc. Also, if you join using #2 you will have to pay all membership fees when you apply.

# Chapter Fourteen

# Summary

It's difficult to put life experiences into information a dancer can use, but I feel any dancer reading this book can see the common threads that every choreographer, entertainment director and dance agent find invaluable.

## CLASS AND TRAINING

Everyone stresses the importance of training. If you're living in your home town and thinking about relocating to N.Y. or LA, please take their advice to heart. Get the best training you can possibly get. After you relocate, everyone agrees that taking class is the only way to survive. It will keep you sharp, help you learn new styles and it's where you'll make most of your connections. If you're thinking you can get by with the training you have – forget it! Not only is the competition severe, but the people holding the auditions can spot a well trained dancer in a count of eight.

## VERSATILITY

In today's entertainment market, is anything more important? Remember our experts' advice, "Don't limit yourself." A versatile dancer is a hot commodity. If you're a street dancer, add some technique training. If you're a classically trained dancer, work on vocals. You never know when you're going to need it. I've had to roller skate in industrials and perform stunt fighting in a Vegas revue. Versatility is a key to making money. Everyone agrees, don't limit yourself.

## ATTITUDE

Who trains for that! It comes from knowing who you are, what you want and treating others with respect. You've heard everyone interviewed say that you'll be evaluated on your attitude as much as your dance ability, and sometimes more. Attitude is not only how you treat your employers, but how you treat other dancers. I told you earlier dancers love to talk and the dance community is very small. I remember dancing in a show where the producers called a meeting and asked the cast about a particular dancer they were considering. Over half the cast had worked with this dancer before, found her difficult to work with and asked the producers not to hire her. She was never hired. Attitude is also how you feel about yourself. You'll need a confident, positive attitude to be able to handle the severe ups and downs of a dance career.

## DIFFICULTY

To become a professional dancer is so difficult I can't even begin to put it into words. I think it's safe to say that every dancer, even the very successful ones, never dreamed it would be so hard. The number of dancers competing for every job is staggering. The economy in the arts is high priced and very risky. A Broadway show carries a five to ten million dollar budget. Dance jobs are on the decline. And if that wasn't enough, you've chosen a career that has a limited length. Everyone agrees, don't go into the arts unless you have ability, talent, training and a passion that won't allow you to do anything else.

If you have to dance—and believe me, I understand the feeling—then do it!

Take your training, your versatility and your good attitude, and give it your best shot. There's nothing more rewarding than beating the odds and being paid for something you love to do.

I wish you the best!

# Index

# ORDER FORM

## Rafter Publishing

11333 Moorpark Street
Suite 141
Toluca Lake, California 91602

Please send me _____ copy(s) of
"Dancing... for a living - two"
I understand that if I'm not 100% satisfied I can return
the book in good condition for a full refund.  I've enclosed
a check/money order payable to
Rafter Publishing.

**Book(s) Price** ........................... $_____
( _____ copies X $19.95)
**Shipping & Handling** ................ $_____
($3.00 – first book,
$1.00 – ea. addl. book)
**CA Sales Tax** ........................... $_____
($1.65 per book
CA residents only)
**TOTAL ENCLOSED** ............. $_____

We will ship your order as soon as possible.
Please allow four to six weeks for delivery.

**$19.95 Softcover**